William Spottiswoode

Catalogue of mercantile, marine and naval models in the South Kensington Museum : with classified table of contents and an alphabetical index of subjects.

William Spottiswoode

Catalogue of mercantile, marine and naval models in the South Kensington Museum : with classified table of contents and an alphabetical index of subjects.

ISBN/EAN: 9783741172649

Manufactured in Europe, USA, Canada, Australia, Japa

Cover: Foto ©Andreas Hilbeck / pixelio.de

Manufactured and distributed by brebook publishing software (www.brebook.com)

William Spottiswoode

Catalogue of mercantile, marine and naval models in the South Kensington Museum : with classified table of contents and an alphabetical index of subjects.

𝔖cience and 𝔄rt 𝔇epartment
of the 𝔈ommittee of 𝔈ouncil on 𝔈ducation.

CATALOGUE

OF

MERCANTILE MARINE AND NAVAL MODELS

IN THE

SOUTH KENSINGTON MUSEUM.

WITH

CLASSIFIED TABLE OF CONTENTS, AND AN
ALPHABETICAL INDEX OF SUBJECTS.

LONDON:
PRINTED BY GEORGE E. EYRE AND WILLIAM SPOTTISWOODE,
PRINTERS TO THE QUEEN'S MOST EXCELLENT MAJESTY.
FOR HER MAJESTY'S STATIONERY OFFICE.

1874.

The Director of the South Kensington Museum will be glad to receive any communications in reference to corrections or additional information for insertion in the next Edition of this Catalogue, addressed to him at the South Kensington Museum, London, S.W., and marked " Marine Gallery."

SCIENCE AND ART DEPARTMENT
OF THE COMMITTEE OF COUNCIL ON EDUCATION.

SOUTH KENSINGTON.

ESTABLISHED in connexion with the Board of Trade in March 1853 as a development of the Department of Practical Art, which in 1852 had been created for the re-organisation of Schools of Design. Placed under the direction of the Committee of Council on Education in 1856.

List of Presidents and Vice-Presidents.

Board of Trade.
1852. Rt. Hon. J. W. Henley, M.P., President.
1853. Rt. Hon. Edwd. Cardwell, M.P.
1855. Rt. Hon. Lord Stanley of Alderley.

Committee of Council on Education.
1856. Rt. Hon. Earl Granville, K.G., Lord President.
" Rt.Hon.W.E. Cowper,M.P.,Vice-President.
1858. Most Hon. Marquess of Salisbury, K.G.
" Rt. Hon. Sir C. B. Adderley, K.C.M.G., M.P.

1859. Rt. Hon. Earl Granville, K.G.
" Rt. Hon. Robert Lowe, M.P.
1864. Rt. Hon. H. A. Bruce, M.P., Vice-President.
1866. His Grace the Duke of Buckingham and Chandos.
" Rt. Hon. H. T. Lowry Corry, M.P.
1867. His Grace the Duke of Marlborough, K.G.
" Rt. Hon. Lord Robert Montagu, M.P.
1868. Most Hon. the Marquess of Ripon, K.G.
" Rt. Hon. W. E. Forster, M.P.
1873. Rt. Hon. Lord Aberdare.
" Rt. Hon. W. E. Forster, M.P., V.P.

Lord President.
His Grace the Duke of Richmond, K.G.

Vice-President of the Committee of Council on Education.
The Right Hon. the Viscount Sandon, M.P.

OFFICE HOURS, TEN TO FOUR.

GENERAL ADMINISTRATION.
Secretary.—Sir Francis R. Sandford, C.B.
Assistant Secretary.—Norman MacLeod.
Chief Clerk.—G. Francis Duncombe.
First-class Clerks.—A. J. R. Trendell; Alan S. Cole; F. R. Fowke; A. S. Bury.
Second-class Clerks.—J. B. Rundell; H. W. Williams; E. Belshaw; G. G. Millard; A. F. E. Torrens; O. J. Dullea.
Postal Clerk.—W. Burtt.
Clerk of Accounts.—Vacant.
Book-keeper.—T. A. Bowler.
Assistant Book-keeper.—E. Harris.

GENERAL STORES.
Storekeeper.—W. G. Groser, *Deputy.*—H. Lloyd.
Clerk.—J. Smith.

SCIENCE DIVISION.
Director.—Major Donnelly, R.E.
Occasional Inspectors.—F. J. Sidney, LL.D.
Capt. Harris, E.I.C. (*Navigation*).
Official Examiner.—G. C. T. Bartley.
Assistant Professional Examiner.—T. Healey.

Professional Examiners for Science.
Subjects.
I.—Practical, plane, and solid Geometry.—Professor F. A. Bradley.
II.—Machine Construction and Drawing.—W. C. Unwin, B.Sc.
III.—Building Construction.—Colonel Wray, R.E.
IV.—Naval Architecture.— W. B. Baskcomb.
V.—Pure Mathematics.—C. W. Merrifield, F.R.S.; T. Savage, M.A.
VI.—Theoretical Mechanics.—Rev. John F. Twisden, M.A.
VII.—Applied Mechanics. — J. Anderson, LL.D., C.E.
VIII.—Acoustics, Light, and Heat.—J. Tyndall, LL.D., F.R.S.
IX.—Magnetism and Electricity.—J. Tyndall, LL.D., F.R.S.

Subjects.
X.—Inorganic Chemistry.—E. Frankland, D.C.L., Ph.D., F.R.S.
XI.—Organic Chemistry.—E. Frankland, D.C.L., Ph.D., F.R.S.
XII.—Geology.—A. C. Ramsay, LL.D., F.R.S.
XIII.—Mineralogy.—W. W. Smyth, M.A. F.R.S.
XIV.—Animal Physiology.—T. H. Huxley, LL.D., F.R.S.
XV.—Elementary Botany.—W. T. T. Dyer, M.A., B.Sc.
XVI.} —General Biology.—T. H. Huxley,
XVII.} LL.D., F.R.S.; W. T. T. Dyer, M.A., B.Sc.
XVIII.—Mining.—W. W. Smyth, M.A., F.R.S.
XIX.—Metallurgy.—J. Percy, M.D., F.R.S.
XX.—Navigation.—J. Woolley, LL.D.
XXI.—Nautical Astronomy.—J. Woolley, LL.D.
XXII.—Steam.—T. M. Goodeve, M.A.
XXIII.—Physical Geography.—D. T. Ansted, M.A., F.R.S.

ART DIVISION.
Inspector-General for Art.—Richard Redgrave, R.A.
Official Inspector for Art.—H. A. Bowler.
Occasional Inspectors.—S. A. Hart, R.A.; F. B. Barwell; W. B. Scott.
Official Examiner.—T. Chesman, B.A., LL.B.
Professional Examiners.—Sir F. Grant, P.R.A.; Sir M. Digby Wyatt; J. C. Horsley, R.A.; F. Leighton, R.A.; F. R. Pickersgill, R.A. C. W. Cope, R.A.; H. Weekes, R.A.; E. J. Poynter, A.R.A.; J. Marshall, F.R.S., F.R.C.S.
Occasional Examiners.—G. M. Atkinson; G. R. Redgrave,

Inspectors of Local Schools of Science and Art.
—R. G. Wylde; J. F Iselin, M.A. E. P. Bartlett.

Organising Master of Science and Art Classes.
—J. C. Buckmaster, F.C.S.

34857.   A 2

SOUTH KENSINGTON MUSEUM.

Director.—P. Cunliffe Owen.
Assistant Directors.—R. A. Thompson; Major E. R. Festing, R.E.
Inspector-General for Art.—Richard Redgrave, R.A.
Director of New Buildings.—Major-Gen. Scott, C.B.
Decorative Artists.—J. Gamble; R. Townroe; F. W. Moody, *Instructor in Decorative Art.*
Editor of Catalogues and Referee for Libraries. —J. H. Pollen, M.A., late Fellow of Merton College, Oxford.
Museum Keeper (Art Collections).—G. Wallis.
Museum Keeper (National Art Library).—R. H. Soden Smith, M.A., Trinity College, Dublin, F.S.A.
Museum Keeper (Educational Library and Collections).—A. C. King, F.S.A.
Assistant Museum Keepers.—W. Matchwick, F.L.S.; H. Sandham; R. Laskey; C. B. Worsnop; R. F. Sketchley, B.A., Exeter College, Oxford; H. E. Acton; J. W. Appell, Ph.D.; T. Clack; J. Barrett, B.A.; C. H. Derby, B.A.
Provisional Assistant Keeper.—C. T. Townshend.
Museum Clerks.—M. Webb; H. M. Cundall.
Provisional Assistants.— H. Vernon; A. Masson; W. E. Streatfeild; F. Coles; W. G. Johnson; G. H. Wallis.
Superintendent of Examples and Publications. —J. Cundall.

NATIONAL ART TRAINING SCHOOL.

Head Master.—Richard Burchett.
Deputy Head Master.—R. W. Herman.
Mechanical and Architectural Drawing.— H. B. Hagreen.
Geometry and Perspective.—E. S. Burchett.
Painting, Freehand Drawing of Ornament, &c., the Figure and Anatomy, and Ornamental Design.—R. Burchett; R. W. Herman; W. Denby; R. Collinson; C. P. Slocombe.
Modelling.—F. M. Miller.
Lady Superintendent of Female Students.— Miss Trulock.
Female Teachers.—Mrs. S. E. Casabianca; Miss Channon.
Lecturer on Anatomy.—Vacant.
Teacher of Etching Class. — T. O. Barlow, A.E.R.A.

BETHNAL GREEN BRANCH OF THE SOUTH KENSINGTON MUSEUM.
(Opened on June 24, 1872.)

GEOLOGICAL SURVEY.

Director-General.—A. C. Ramsay, LL.D., F.R.S.
Director for England and Wales. — H. W. Bristow, F.R.S.
Director for Ireland.—E. Hull, M.A., F.R.S.
Director for Scotland.—A. Geikie, F.R.S.
Naturalist.—T. H. Huxley, LL.D., F.R.S.
Palæontologist.—R. Etheridge.

ROYAL SCHOOL OF MINES AND MUSEUM OF PRACTICAL GEOLOGY.

Director.—
Keeper of Mining Records. — Robert Hunt, F.R.S.
Assistants.—Richard Meade; James B. Jordan.

Registrar, Curator, and Librarian.—T. Reeks.
Assistant Librarian.—T. Newton.
Assistant Curator.—F. W. Rudler.

PROFESSORS.

Chemistry.—Edward Frankland, D.C.L., Ph.D., F.R.S.
Natural History.—T. H. Huxley, LL.D., F.R.S.
Physics.—F. Guthrie, B.A., Ph.D.
Applied Mechanics.—T. M. Goodeve, M.A.
Metallurgy.—J. Percy, M.D., F.R.S.
Geology.—A. C. Ramsay, LL.D., F.R.S.
Mining and Mineralogy.—W. W. Smyth, M.A., F.R.S.
Mechanical Drawing.—Rev. J. H. Edgar, M.A.

Museum open every week-day but Friday, and on Saturdays and Mondays till 10 p.m., except from the 10th of August to the 10th of September.

EDINBURGH MUSEUM OF SCIENCE AND ART.

Director.—Prof. T. C. Archer, F.R.S.E.
Keeper of Natural History Collections.— R. H. Traquair, M.D.
Curator.—Alexander Galletly.
Assistant in Natural History Museum.—J. Gibson.
Assistant in Industrial Museum.—J. Paton.
Clerks.—J. Gibson; W. Clark.

ROYAL COLLEGE OF SCIENCE, DUBLIN.

Dean of Faculty.—R. Galloway.
Secretary.—F. J. Sidney, LL.D.
Curator of Museum.—A. Gages.
Clerk.—G. C. Penny.

PROFESSORS.

Physics.—W. F. Barrett, F.C.S.
Chemistry.—R. Galloway.
Geology.—E. Hull, M.A., F.R.S.
Applied Mathematics.—
Botany.—W. R. McNab, M.D.
Zoology.—H. A. Nicholson, M.A., M.D., D.Sc.
Agriculture.—E. W. Davy, M.B.
Descriptive Geometry and Drawing.—Thomas F. Pigot.
Mining and Mineralogy.—J. P. O'Reilly.
Demonstrator in Palæontology.—W. H. Baily, F.L.S.
Assistant Chemist.—W. Plunkett.

ROYAL DUBLIN SOCIETY.

President.— His Excellency the Lord Lieutenant.
Secretaries.—G. W. Maunsell, A.M.; Lawrence Waldron, D.L.
Registrar and Assistant Secretary. — W. E. Steele, M.D.
Treasurer, &c.—H. C. White.
Director of Natural History Museum.—A. Carte, M.D.
Keeper of Minerals.—Dr. J. Emerson Reynolds.
Librarian.—E. R. P. Collis.
Temporary Assistant—H. W. D. Dunlop.
Director of Botanic Gardens, Glasnevin.—D. Moore, Ph.D.

ZOOLOGICAL GARDENS, DUBLIN.

Secretaries.—Professor M'Dowel, M.D.; Rev. S. Haughton, M.D., F.R.S.

CATALOGUE OF THE COLLECTION

OF

Mercantile Marine and Naval Models in the South Kensington Museum.

PREFACE.

THE present collection of Models of ships of the Mercantile Marine, and Ships of War, has been acquired by loans and gifts from private sources to the South Kensington Museum, since the formation, in 1864, of a collection of ship Models illustrating naval architecture and marine engineering.

On the removal to Greenwich in 1873 of the collection of naval models belonging to the Admiralty it was determined to continue, as part of the collections of the South Kensington Museum, an exhibition of the Models of ships and tackle in connexion with them, acquired from time to time by the Science and Art Department of the Committee of Council on Education; which now form a tolerably complete series.

To the Models of ships are added Models and Drawings of steam-engines applied to the propulsion of ships by screw propellers or paddle wheels, also of marine steam boilers, engine and boiler accessories, as well as various other illustrations of steamship machinery in general.

A valuable nucleus thus exists for the study of the science of marine architecture and engineering.

The following are amongst the principal objects in the collection:—

A series of whole and half block Models of proposed armour plated ships of war, presented in 1867 by Messrs. R. Napier & Sons, of Glasgow.

A series of Models of merchant and war ships built from time to time by them, lent by Messrs. Laird, Brothers, Birkenhead.

A series of whole and half block Models of ocean steamships, lent by Messrs. W. Denny & Brothers, of Dumbarton.

A series of steamship Models, lent by the Palmer's Shipbuilding Co., Limited, Newcastle.

Models of the engines of H.M.S. "MONARCH." and "PRINCE ALBERT," lent by Messrs. Humphrys and Tennant, of Deptford.

Models of paddle wheel and screw propeller engines, lent by Messrs. Ravenhill, Easton, & Co., London.

Steam - engine and boiler accessories, lent by Messrs. Schäffer & Budenberg, of Magdeburg, Manchester, and London.

Great assistance has been received from many private ship-building and engineering firms in forming the present collection of Marine Models for public instruction in London.

The annexed account of the history of the "Navy office" or present Admiralty, taken from the preface to the catalogue of the models lately exhibited by the Admiralty in the South Kensington Museum, may perhaps be found interesting.

H. SANDHAM.

October 1874.

The following short historical sketch of the Navy Office, extracted chiefly from the 5th Report of the Commissioners of Inquiry, dated 14th February 1788, (page 25) contain some very interesting information :—

"The records of the office do not furnish us with any information further back than July 1660, but we understand that the first establishment of Royal Navy office was in the reign of King Henry VIII., who appointed certain officers, under the title of principal officers of his navy, to manage the civil branches thereof, under the Lord High Admiral ; but these officers had no positive instructions for their guidance in the execution of their duty until the reign of Edward VI., when certain ordinances were issued for the conduct of the officers entrusted with the management of the marine affairs, which ordinances form the basis of all later instructions given for the conduct of the officers to whom the management of the civil branches of the Navy was committed. The officers at that time appointed to this duty were the Vice-Admiral of the Fleet, the Master of the Ordnance, the Surveyor of Marine Causes, the Treasurer, the Controller, the General Surveyor of the Victualling, the Clerk of the Ships, and the Clerk of the Stores, who were directed to meet once a week at the office on Tower Hill, to consult together for the good order of the Navy, and to report their proceedings once a month to the High Admiral ; particular duties were also assigned to each member.

"The affairs of the Navy appear to have continued under the management of such officers until the time of King James I., who, in the sixteenth year of his reign, issued a commission under the great seal to Sir Thomas Smith and others, to inquire into the frauds and abuses which had been committed in the Navy, with power to remedy the same, and to manage, settle, and put the officers of the Navy into a right course. This commission was determined upon the demise of King James I. in 1625, when his successor, King Charles I., issued a new commission to the same persons. By this commission the offices of the controller and surveyor were suspended during its continuance, and the same continued in force until the year 1628, when it was made void by a new commission, restoring the management of the affairs of the Navy to the ancient principal officers established in the reign of King Edward VI. ; but between this time and breaking out of the Civil War several commissions appear to have been issued for regulating and settling the affairs of the Navy, during the continuance of which the functions of the original principal officers were always suspended.

"Upon the restoration of King Charles II. his Majesty constituted a Navy Board, by commission under the great seal, consisting of the Treasurer, Controller, Surveyor, and Clerk of the Navy, who were styled principal officers, to whom, on the 4th July 1660, three commissioners were added, to assist the said principal officers in the management of the affairs of the Navy.

"In January 1661 the Duke of York (then Lord High Admiral) established certain instructions now in use (1778) for the conduct of the four principal officers ; the other three being commissioners at large, had no particular line of duty allotted to them until the year 1666, when one of them was directed to take upon him so much of the controller's duty as related to the examination and and control of the treasurer's accounts; another that part related to victualling accounts; and in the year 1671, the third commissioner had that part of the controller's duty which related to the examination and control of the storekeeper's accounts, assigned to him, which, with the addition of one commissioner at large, is the present (1778) arrangement of the Navy Board."

In consequence of the great increase of the Navy, these arrangements were found incomplete and insufficient to insure the strict investigation and examination of accounts, the direction and proper conduct of correspondence and supervision of stores; instead of the commissioners presiding over separate departments, committees were formed, and the business divided so as to admit of competent officers in each branch, possessing time and opportunity, to examine, digest, and conduct the parts allotted to them. Under this idea, by Order in Council of 8th June 1796, the Navy Board was divided into the three following committees:—

A Committee of Correspondence.
A Committee of Accounts.
A Committee of Stores.

The controller to belong to and preside at every committee.

The designing, building, and repair of ships was in the hands of the surveyors, of whom at one time there were three, and generally two, under the presidency of the controller.

In the year 1796 the Board consisted of the following members, viz.:—Sir Andrew Snape Hamond, Bart., Controller; Charles Hope, Esq., Deputy Controller; Sir John Henslowe and Sir W. Rule, Surveyors; George Marsh, Esq., George Rogers, Esq., William Palmer, Esq., Sir William Bellingham, Bart., Harry Harwood, Esq., and Samuel Gambier, Esq.

The office of Deputy Controller was abolished in the year 1816. In the following year the Transport Board, created in 1793, was broken up, and a Transport Committee was formed at the Navy Board.

A surveyor was reduced in 1822, and a civil commissioner in the same year, leaving at the Board the following persons, viz.:— one Comptroller, two Surveyors, three Naval Officers, and three Civil Commissioners, in the whole nine, and thus employed :— Two at the Committee of Correspondence, two at the Committee of Accounts, two at the Committee of Stores, two at the Committee of Transport, with the controller at the head of each.

In 1832, during the presidence of Sir James Graham at the Board of Admiralty, the Navy Board was abolished, the civil affairs of the Navy being for the future conducted by the principal officers, under the direct control of the Board of Admiralty. At that time the department charged with the design and construction of ships consisted of a Surveyor (a naval officer) and two Assistant Surveyors. In 1857 this department was placed under a Controller (a naval officer), one Chief Constructor, and one Constructor, to which staff an Assistant Constructor was added in 1861. In 1864, by Order in Council, the constitution of the office was altered to a Controller, a Chief Constructor, and three Assistant Constructors.

The several Royal Dockyards were established as under :—

Deptford -	- Early in the reign of Henry VIII. Closed April 1869.
Woolwich	- Called by Camden the Mother Dockyard, in the reign of Henry VIII., about 1509. Closed October 1st, 1869.
Chatham -	- In the reign of Queen Elizabeth on the site of the present gun wharf; removed to the present site about the year 1622.

Sheerness	- Established in the reign of Charles II., about 1661. The present dockyard and basins were completed about the year 1823.
Portsmouth	- In the reign of Henry VIII. In 1666, a dry dock and the Commissioner's house were built; and in 1848 the steam factory and steam basin were formed.
Plymouth	- Prior to 1691, the Master Shipwright and workmen were borne on board of a ship fitted for their reception; and in 1693, in the reign of William and Mary, the dockyard was completed. In the year 1824, the name was changed from Plymouth Dock to Devonport.
Milford	- A temporary yard, prior to 1815, at which time it was removed to Pater Hobb's Point, and is now known as Pembroke Dockyard.

CLASSIFICATION

Of the Collection of MERCANTILE MARINE and NAVAL MODELS in the SOUTH KENSINGTON MUSEUM.

Class I. Whole MODELS—rigged and unrigged—Representing lines and forms of sailing ships and steam ships. Page 10.

Class II. Half-block MODELS of sailing ships and steam ships, showing lines and forms. Page 22.

Class III. MODELS of construction. Sailing ships and steam ships, wood and iron.—Keels, timbers, frames, beams, knees, &c. Sectional models. Page 28.

Class IV. MODELS of fitments. Cabins and their fittings. Ports, skylights, hatchways, ladders, &c.—Ventilation of ships. Fire hearths (cooking), cabin stoves. Page 41.

Class V. APPLIANCES used in ships. Capstans and windlasses. Tanks, pumps, &c. Anchors and chain cables, and gear connected with them. Page 43.

Class VI. MASTS. Rigging, standing and running. Sails. Page 44.

Class VII. METHODS OF PROPULSION. Oars and sculls, sweeps. Steam engines and boilers. Screw propellers, paddle wheels, &c. Page 48.

Class VIII. STEERING APPARATUS. Rudders, permanent and temporary. Steering gear of all kinds, manual and steam power. Page 55.

Class IX. BOATS. Ships' boats. Life-boats and rafts. All kinds of boats and barges used for pleasure. Page 57.

Class X. INSTRUMENTS FOR NAVIGATION. Compasses, logs, chronometers, sextants, &c. Barometers. Nautachometers, clinometers, &c. Signal flags and ships' lights. Page 64.

Class XI. GUNS. Breech and muzzle loading guns. Shot and shell. Gun carriages. Batteries, turrets, &c. Page 66.

Class XII. MODELS of home vessels. Fishing and pilot boats. Sailing and steam barges, hoys, lighters. Canal boats. River steam boats. Pleasure yachts. Page 73.

Class XIII. FOREIGN CRAFT and Vessels, of all kinds. Page 74.

Class XIV. PAINTINGS, drawings, and photographs, of ships; and of subjects in connexion with them. Page 76.

Class XV. Miscellaneous MODELS, and objects not comprised in the foregoing classes. Page 92.

CLASS I.

Whole Models—rigged and unrigged—showing Lines and Forms of Sailing Ships and Steam Ships.

1. WHOLE MODEL, full rigged, of H.M.S. "RACOON," (on a $\frac{3}{10}$-in. scale), 22 guns, 400 horse-power.
Lent by H.R.H. the Duke of Edinburgh. 1865.
Note.—The "RACOON," 22 guns, 400 horse-power, length 200 ft. 1 in., breadth 40 ft. 4 in., depth 22 ft. 8 in., tonnage 1,467, was laid down at Chatham Yard in April 1856. Launched in April 1857. Designed by Surveyor's Department, Admiralty.
There were also built on the same lines the "Challenger," at Woolwich in 1858, and the "Clio," at Sheerness in 1858.
The armament was as as follows:

No.	Prs.	Weight.	Length.
		cwt.	ft. in.
20	8-in.	60	8 10
2	68-pr. pivot	95	10 0
22 Total.			

The complement of men was 280.

2. WHOLE MODEL, full rigged, of H.M.S. "NORTHUMBERLAND," (iron), 26 guns, 1,350 horse-power, screw (on a ¼-in. scale). Length 400 ft., breadth 59 ft. 3½ in., depth 21 ft. 1 in., tonnage 6,621. Building now (1865) by contract at Millwall, by the Millwall Iron Works and Shipbuilding Company. She was commenced by Messrs. C. J. Mare & Co., at their Yard at Millwall in October 1861. Designed by the Controller's Department, Admiralty.
There were also built on the same lines the "Minotaur" and "Agincourt,"
The armament is—

	No.	Prs.	
Main deck	{ 4	300	12-ton guns.
	{ 18	100	6½ "
Upper "	4	100	6½ "
	Total 26		

CLASS I.—WHOLE MODELS.   11

Note.—This MODEL, showing three masts and 50 guns, was made before the masting and armament of the ship had been decided on. The ship now has five masts and 26 guns.
Lent by the Millwall Iron Works Company. 1865.

3. WHOLE MODEL, full rigged, of H.M.S. "AJAX" (on a $\frac{1}{2}$-in. scale), 64 guns, tonnage 1,953. Laid down at Messrs. Randall's yard, on the Thames, in 1795, launched in 1798, burnt in 1807.
This model was constructed by the late Sir Joseph Sydney Yorke, Bart., between the years 1797 and 1808.
Presented by the Earl of Hardwicke. 1865.

4. WHOLE MODEL of a design for a four-decked ship of war, "Duke of Kent," to carry 170 guns.
Proposed by Mr. Joseph Tucker in 1809, when Master Shipwright of Plymouth Dockyard.
Lent by Mr. J. S. Tucker. 1865.
See also Class III., p. 30, No. 8.

4A. SERIES OF MODELS, presented in 1867, by Messrs. R. Napier & Sons, Glasgow, illustrating a system of proposals and plans for combined Turret and Broadside navies, by the late Vice-Admiral Edward Pellew Halsted, R.N.
The ships, designed by C. F. Henwood, Esq., Naval Architect, are fitted on the turret and iron tripod mast system of the late Captain Cowper P. Coles, R.N., C.B.
The guns proposed for the armament of these ships, are wholly constructed and rifled on the principle for heavy ordnance of Sir Joseph Whitworth, Bart.; and are mounted upon the muzzle-pivoting gun carriages designed by Captain T. B. Heathorn, R.A.
See Whitworth projectiles, Class XI., No. 3, pp. 67, 68.

a. WHOLE MODEL, full-rigged, of the proposed ship-of-war "DREADNOUGHT," classed as a first-rate. 7 Turrets.
Turrets   -   -   - 7
Number of guns in turrets   - 14 of 9-inch calibre.
Number of broadside guns   - 4 of 7-inch calibre.
    and   -   -   - 10 of 4-inch   „
Tonnage, 10,764, builder's old measurement.
Nominal horse-power, 1,300.
Length of ship, 455 feet. Breadth, 70 feet.
Depth, 28 feet. Load draught, 26 feet 6 inches.
Designed May 1866. Scale, $\frac{1}{4}$ inch to 1 foot.

12   CATALOGUE OF MARINE MODELS.

Note.—The masts and rigging of this model illustrate the following conditions :—
Foremast : shows the mast as it would appear when "prepared for action," and ship steaming head to wind.
Mainmast : represents the position of the yards and sails when " sailing close hauled."
Mizenmast : represents the yards squared and dressed, ship lying in harbour.

b. WHOLE MODEL, full-rigged, of the proposed ship-of-war "ACTIVE," classed as a corvette or 6th rate. 2 Turrets.
Turrets - - - 2
Number of guns in turrets - 4 of 9-inch calibre.
Number of broadside guns - 10 of 7-inch „
Tonnage, 4,926, builder's old measurement.
Nominal horse-power, 1,000.
Length of ship, 367 feet 6 inches. Breadth, 52 feet 6 inches. Depth, 25 feet.
Load draught, 24 feet 6 inches.
Designed May 1866. Scale, $\frac{1}{4}$ inch to 1 foot.
Note.—The yards on the masts of this model show the ship as "running before the wind."

c. WHOLE MODEL, unrigged, of the proposed ship-of-war or ocean despatch vessel "VEDETTE," classed as an 8th-rate ship. 1 Turret.
Turret - - - 1
Number of guns in turret - 2 of 9-inch calibre.
Number of broadside guns - 10 of $5\frac{1}{2}$ inch „
Tonnage, 3,648, builder's old measurement.
Displacement, 5,700 tons.
Nominal horse-power, 800.
Length of ship, 332 feet 6 inches. Breadth, 47 feet 6 inches. Depth, 23 feet.
Load draught, 22 feet 6 inches.
Designed May 1866. Scale, $\frac{1}{4}$ inch to 1 foot.
The Models *a., b., c., d.*, presented by Messrs. R. Napier & Sons, Glasgow.   1867.

See also Half block Models, No. 57, Class II., p. 23.

5. WHOLE MODEL of a proposed armour-plated frigate with two batteries, carrying 6 heavy rifled guns in each, besides 28 broadside guns.
Length of ship, 444 feet.
Designed by Mr. George Turner, late Master Shipwright, Woolwich Dockyard.   Lent 1864.

6. WHOLE MODEL of a proposed armour-plated frigate, carrying a battery of 8 heavy rifled guns and 14 broadside guns.
Length of ship, 330 feet.
Designed by Mr. George Turner, late Master Shipwright, Woolwich Dockyard.
Lent 1864.

7. WHOLE MODEL of a proposed armour-plated corvette, carrying a battery of 4 heavy rifled guns and 4 broadside guns.
Length of ship, 210 feet.
Designed by Mr. George Turner, late Master Shipwright, Woolwich Dockyard.
Lent 1864.

8. WHOLE MODEL of H.M.S. "CHESTER," 50 guns. Built at Chatham or Woolwich, about 1670.
Lent by Mr. J. Dafforne. 1869.

9. WHOLE MODEL, brig rigged, of a proposed ironclad war vessel, with turret and battery combined, on a system proposed and designed by Mr. R. Dawson.
The vessel represents a ship 316 feet long, 66 feet beam, 4,000 tons. Draught of water, 20 feet; freeboard, 16 feet.
Presented by Mr. R. Dawson. 1870.

10. WHOLE MODEL of an armour-plated frigate, illustrating Mr. R. Griffith's proposals for improved screw propulsion. The ship is fitted with a bow and stern screw propeller placed well under the ship, and working in circular tunnels.
Note.—The chief objects desired by this system for ship propulsion are:—Increase of speed, and economy of fuel. Protection to the screws. No vibration from the propellers. Reduction in size of engines and screws. Increased facility for manœuvring the vessel. In case of disablement to either screw, propelling power is available from the other.
Proposed by Mr. R. Griffiths in 1872, and lent by him. 1874.

11. WHOLE MODEL of the 74-gun French ship-of-war "LE SCEPTRE." Date about 1700–1750. Full-rigged. No sails.
Purchased from Mr. G. Broker. 1871.

12. WHOLE MODEL, fully rigged, of the Imperial French steam screw yacht "JEROME NAPOLEON," built at Cherbourg, 18 . Lent 1872.

Note.—The details of this model, the hull, deck fittings, ships' boats, masts, rigging, and sails, are executed with the minutest care and exactness, and are vivid representations of the several originals on board the yacht itself.

Lent by H.I.H. the Prince Napoleon.   1872.

See Photograph, Class XIV., No. 85, p. 90.

13. WHOLE MODEL of the Trinity House paddle steam yacht "GALATEA." Tons 507 B.M. Nominal horse-power 200. Makers of the engines, Messrs. Laird, Brothers, Birkenhead. Launched in 1867. Built by Messrs. Caird and Company, Greenock.

Lent by the Corporation of the Trinity House. 1869.

14. WHOLE MODEL of the Turkish iron armour-clad screw frigates "OSMANEA," "AZIZEA," and "ORKHANEA." Length 293 ft., beam 36 ft., tonnage 4,222, builders' measurement, guns 42, nominal horse-power 900. Constructed for the Imperial Ottoman Government by R. Napier & Sons.

Presented by Messrs. R. Napier & Sons, Glasgow. 1867.

15. WHOLE MODEL of a design for an armour-plated war vessel, on the turret principle. Submitted to the Admiralty in 1862. Length 365 ft., breadth 60 ft., tons 6,300, horse-power 1,160, speed 15 knots, guns 22.

Lent by Messrs. Westwood & Baillie, Isle of Dogs, Poplar.   1865.

16. WHOLE MODEL of H.M.'s Indian relief, steam troopship "JUMNA." Built 1866, by Palmer's Shipbuilding Company, Limited, Newcastle. Length 365 ft., breadth 48 ft. 9 in., depth 42 ft., tonnage gross 4,174, horse-power 700 nominal, speed 14½ knots per hour. Scale 1-48th full size.

Lent by the Palmer's Shipbuilding Company, Limited, Newcastle-on-Tyne.   1874.

Note.—There were also built on the same lines, about the same time, the "MALABAR," by Messrs. Napier & Sons, the "CROCODILE," by Messrs. Wigram, the "SERAPIS," by the Thames Iron Shipbuilding Company, and the "EUPHRATES," built of iron, 700 horse-power. A class of five to form a direct service for the transport of troops to and fro between England and India. Length of the "EUPHRATES" 360 ft., breadth 49 ft., draught 19 ft. forward, 21 ft. aft, tonnage 4,206, speed 14·718 knots. Built by contract by Messrs. Laird, Brothers. Laid down in May 1865, launched November 1866. Designed by the Controller's Department, Admiralty.

CLASS I.—WHOLE MODELS. 15

17. WHOLE MODEL of the mail screw steamer "MON-"TANA," Liverpool and New York line. Built 1873, by the Palmer's Shipbuilding Company, Limited. Length 412 ft., breadth 43½ ft., depth 42¾ ft., tonnage gross 4,320 horse-power 900 nominal, speed 15¼ knots per hour. Scale 1-48th full size.
 Lent by the Palmer's Shipbuilding Company, Limited, Newcastle-on-Tyne. 1874.

18. WHOLE MODEL of the mail screw steamer "BRIN-"DISI," Ancona and Alexandria line. Built by the Palmer's Shipbuilding Company, Limited. Length 260 ft., breadth 28 ft., depth 21½ ft., tonnage gross 900, horse-power 180 nominal, speed 13 knots per hour. Scale 1-48th full size.
 Lent by the Palmer's Shipbuilding Company, Limited, Newcastle-on-Tyne. 1874.
 See also No. 64, Class II., Page 26.

19. Series of WHOLE MODELS representing various paddle and screw steamships of war and commerce. Designed and built by Messrs. Laird Brothers, engineers and shipbuilders, Birkenhead. Lent 1873.

 WHOLE MODEL of the armour-clad gun-boat "BAHIA." Imperial Brazilian Government. Length 175 ft., breadth 35 ft., depth 11 ft., tons 1,008, draught 8 ft., horse-power 140. Built 1865. Scale ¼ in. to 1 foot.

 WHOLE MODEL of the armour-clad monitor "HEILIGER-"LEE." Royal Dutch navy. Length 180 ft., breadth 44 ft., depth 11 ft. 6 in., tons 1,588, draught 9 ft., horse-power 140. Built 1868. Scale ¼ in. to 1 foot.

 WHOLE MODEL of the screw steam yacht "MORE VANE." Length 57 ft. 5 in., breadth 11 ft., depth 5 ft. 4 in., tons 35, draught 5 ft. 6 in., horse-power 15. Built 1869. Scale ¼ in. to 1 foot.

 WHOLE MODEL of screw steam barge, to carry a 12-pr. howitzer-gun. Length 50 ft., breadth 11 ft., depth 4 ft. 9 in., tons 28, draught 3 ft., horse-power 10. Built 1867. Scale ½ in. to 1 foot.

 WHOLE MODEL of screw steam yacht "LANCASHIRE "WITCH." S. Platt, Esq., owner. Fitted with R. R. Bevis' feathering screw propeller. Length 106 ft. 6 in., breadth 18 ft., depth 9 ft. 6 in., tons 165, draught 7 ft., horse-power 35 ft. Built 1872. Scale ¼ in. to 1 foot.

WHOLE MODEL of the royal mail screw steamers, "SANTA ROSA" and "COLOMBIA." Pacific Steam Navigation Company. Length 300 ft., breadth 32, depth 22 ft. 3 in., tons 2,150, draught 13 ft. 3 in., horse-power 400. Built 1872. Scale ¼ in. to 1 ft.

WHOLE MODEL of the royal mail screw steamer "BRITANNIA." Pacific Steam Navigation Company. Length 399 ft., breadth 43 ft., depth 35 ft. 3 in., tons 3,700, draught 22 ft., horse-power 600. Built 1873. Scale ¼ in. to 1 ft.

See also Drawing, No. 68, Class XIV., Page 87.

WHOLE MODEL of H.M.'s armour-clad turret ship "WIVERN." Length 220 ft., breadth 42 ft., depth 19 ft. 6 in., tons 1,827, draught 15 ft., horse-power 350. Built 1864. Scale ⅛ in. to 1 ft.

Note.—The "WIVERN" (formerly "EL MONASSIR"), iron, shield ship, 4 guns, 350 horse-power, screw, rigged. Built by Messrs. Laird at Birkenhead, launched 1864. There was also built on the same lines the "SCORPION" (formerly "EL TOUSSON,") at Birkenhead at the same time. The armament of H.M.S. "WIVERN" is four 12-ton guns in revolving shields, upon the plan of the late Captain C. P. Coles, R.N., C.B.

WHOLE MODEL of the armour-clad turret ship "DE STIER." Royal Dutch navy. Length 195 ft., breadth 38 ft., depth 19 ft., tons 1,312, draught 15 ft. 6 in., horse-power 350. Built 1868. Scale ¼ in. to 1 ft.

WHOLE MODEL of the light-draught paddle steamer "CRANBORNE," for Indian river steam navigation. Length 213 ft., breadth 28 ft., depth 7 ft. 7 in., tons 819, draught 3 ft. 6 in., horse-power 150. Built 1866. Scale ¼ in. to 1 ft.

WHOLE MODEL of a light-draught paddle steamer for Indian river navigation. Length 90 ft., breadth 15 ft., depth 4 ft., tons 97, draught 2 ft. 2 in., horse-power 30. Built 1871. Scale ¼ in. to 1 ft.

The above 11 models lent by Messrs. Laird Brothers, Birkenhead. 1873.

20. WHOLE MODEL of the merchant ship "CYGNET" on launching ways. The port side built, starboard side showing ship's framing and disposition of timbers. Scale ¼ inch to 1 foot.

Lent by Mr. A. T. Lowe. 1870.

21. WHOLE MODEL of the Light ship stationed on the Goodwin Sands, with lanterns, and all fitments complete for day and night service. Scale ½ inch to 1 foot.

CLASS I.—WHOLE MODELS. 17

Note.—The following are the principal dimensions of the Goodwin Sands Lightship :—
Length 96 ft., breadth 21 ft., depth 10 ft. 8 in. Tons 195.
Height of main globe from water line, 58 ft.
Weight of mushroom (anchor), 42 cwt.
Size of chain cable 1½ in., Length of cable 210 fathoms.
The port side of the vessel shows the ship built complete.
Starboard side shows the timbers, waling, &c.
Lent by the Corporation of the Trinity House.
1865.

22. WHOLE MODEL of the first Iron steamers built on the Thames. The "LORD W. BENTINCK," "MAGNA," and "JUMNA," in 1832, for the Honourable East India Company, for the navigation of the river Ganges. Designed and built by Messrs. Maudslay, Sons, and Field.
Presented by Messrs. Maudslay, Sons, and Field. 1866.

23. WHOLE MODEL of the iron screw steamer "MEDWAY," tons 1,464, nominal horse-power 250. Designed and built by Messrs. Oswald and Co.
This steamer was employed, in conjunction with the "GREAT EASTERN" steamship, in laying the Atlantic telegraph cable, 1866.
Lent by Messrs. Oswald & Co., Sunderland. 1867.

24. WHOLE MODEL of the City of Dublin Steam Packet Company's paddle mail steamer "CONNAUGHT," running between Kingstown and Holyhead. Length 348 ft., width 35 ft., depth 20 ft. 3 in., tonnage 2,039, nominal horse-power 720. Diameter of cylinders 98 inches, length of stroke 6 ft. 6 in. Speed 21 statute miles per hour. Makers of the engines, which are on the oscillating principle, Messrs. Ravenhill, Salkeld, and Co., London. The ship was designed and built by Messrs. John Laird, Sons, and Co., Birkenhead, and launched in 1860.
Lent by Messrs. Laird Brothers, Birkenhead. 1869.

25. MODEL of an Iron Screw Steamer, built and designed by Messrs. Oswald and Co., for the Baltic or Mediterranean trade.
Note.—The principal dimensions of this trading steamer are :—Length over all, 206 feet; breadth, extreme, 28 feet 10 inches; depth, 18 feet 4 inches; tonnage, B.M., 806; Register, gross, 750; draft, light, 7 feet; laden 16 feet; horse-power, 100 nominal; diameter of cylinders, 36 inches; stroke, 26 inches.
Lent by Messrs. Oswald & Co., Sunderland. 1867.

26. WHOLE MODEL of the Woodside ferry paddle steam boat "CHESHIRE," employed between Birkenhead and Liverpool. Licensed to carry 1,620 passengers. Draught of water 6 ft. Designed by Mr. George Harrison, M.I.C.E. The Millwall Iron Works Company. 1864.

27. WHOLE MODEL of the iron sailing ship "DURHAM." Designed and built by Messrs. Oswald & Co. For Messrs. Temperley, Carter, & Co., London.

Note.—The principal dimensions of the sailing ship "DURHAM" are :—Length over all, 209 feet 6 inches; breadth, 34 feet 9 inches; depth, 20 feet 9 inches; tonnage, B.M., 1,131; register, 998; draft, light, 8 feet 2¼ inches; laden, 18 feet 4½ inches; displacement at load line, 1,378 tons.

Lent by Messrs. Oswald & Co., Sunderland. 1867.

28. WHOLE MODEL (on about ¼ inch scale) of the schooner yacht "AMERICA." Length 95 ft., beam 22 ft. Draft forward, 7 feet; aft, 11 feet. Tons 210. Built 1851. Designed by Mr. Steers, New York. Rebuilt by Mr. Henry Pitcher at Northfleet.

Note.—The "AMERICA," yacht, was in America during the early part of the Civil war, 1860–1864, and sunk by the Federals. This is the famous yacht which came over from America in 1851 to challenge the yachts of England, and beat the "TITANIA" 4 minutes and 45 seconds in a run of 20 miles before the wind, and 45 minutes returning by the wind.

The advantage of the "AMERICA" may in some measure be attributed to her having cotton canvas instead of flax, and to the very superior manner in which her sails were cut, together with the fact that her tonnage was about double that of the "TITANIA."

Lent by Mr. John Scott Russell, F.R.S. 1868.

29. WHOLE MODEL of the clipper merchant ship "FIERY CROSS." Built 1861, for the China tea trade, by Chaloner, Hart, and Co., Liverpool. Designed by Mr. Rennie. A previous ship built, 1855, by Messrs. Rennie and Rankill, Liverpool, from designs by Mr. Rennie. Dimensions are as follows:—Extreme length 185 feet, extreme breadth 31 ft. 3 in., depth 19 ft. 6 in. Tonnage, o.m. 363, register 702. Displacement 1,615·84 tons. Scale ¼ in. to 1 ft.

Lent by J. Campbell, Esq. 1869.

See also No. 65, page 26.

CLASS I.—WHOLE MODELS. 19

30. WHOLE MODEL, rigged complete, of a Dutch galiot of the period 1774–1778. The model bears these dates. It is richly carved throughout, specially at the bow and stern, hatchways, leeboards, &c. Length of model 3 ft. 2 in., beam 12 in.
   Purchased from Van Vliet and Co. 1871.

31. WHOLE MODEL of the Cunard iron paddle steamer "SCOTIA." Built 1861. Constructed for the British and North American (Cunard) Royal Mail Steam Packet Company by R. Napier & Sons.
   Note.—The principal dimensions of the paddle steamship "SCOTIA" are:—Length 366 feet, breadth 47 feet 6 inches, tonnage, builder's measurement, 4,050, load displacement 6,520 tons, horse-power 1,000 nominal. Diameter of cylinders 100 inches, length of stroke 12 feet.
   Diameter of paddle wheels, 40 feet.
   Size of floats, 11 feet 6 inches by 2 feet.
   Presented by Messrs. R. Napier & Sons, Glasgow.
                1867.

32. WHOLE MODEL of the Montreal Ocean Steamship Company's screw steamers "HIBERNIAN" and "NORWEGIAN." Designed and built by W. Denny and Brothers, Dumbarton. Scale ¼ inch to 1 foot.
   This model shows on the port side the internal arrangements of cabins, engine-room, &c.
   Note.—The dimensions of the steamships "HIBERNIAN" and "NORWEGIAN" are:—Length of keel and fore rake, 292 feet; breadth, beam, moulded, 37 feet 9 inches; depth, moulded, 33 feet; tonnage, o.m. 2,041; horse-power, 400, nominal.
   Lent by Messrs. W. Denny and Brothers, Dumbarton, N.B. 1865.

33. WHOLE MODEL of the screw steamer "CITY OF PARIS," belonging to the Liverpool, New York, and Philadelphia Steam Shipping Company (*Inman Line*). Tons 2,740, nominal horse-power 550. Launched December 1865.
   Presented by Mr. William Inman, the Inman Company, Liverpool. 1866.

34. WHOLE MODEL of the West India and Pacific Steam Shipping Company's screw steamer "VENEZUELAN." Length 259 feet 5 in., breadth 32 feet 1 in., depth, extreme, 28 feet 9 in. Tons 1,682, horse-power 220. Makers of the

engines, Messrs. Jas. Jack and Company, Liverpool. Launched 1865. Built by Messrs. Jones, Quiggin, and Company, Liverpool.
Lent by the West India and Pacific Steam Shipping Company. 1868.

35. WHOLE MODEL of the West India and Pacific Steam Shipping Company's screw steamer "BOLIVAR." Length 240 feet, breadth 32 feet 5 in., depth 19 feet 7 in. Tons 1,250, horse-power 200. Maker of the engines, J. C. Thompson, Newcastle-on-Tyne. Direct acting inverted cylinder engines; diameter of cylinders, 49 inches. Stroke 2 feet 6 inches. Launched 1862. Built by Messrs. Richardson, Duck, and Company, Stockton-on-Tees.
Lent by the West India and Pacific Steam Shipping Company. 1868.

36. WHOLE MODEL of the blockade-runner paddle wheel steamer " EVELYN." Length 230 ft., breadth of beam 28 ft., draught of water with 1,000 bales of cotton on board 7 ft. Tons 284 N.M.; horse-power 200. Speed at full power, 17 knots. Built in 1864 by Messrs. Randolph, Elder, & Co., Glasgow.
The late Capt. Hugh Talbot Burgoyne, R.N. 1865.

37. WHOLE MODEL of the fore and aft schooner yacht " KALAFISH." 60 tons burden. Designed and built by owner Dr. J. Collis Browne, late Army Medical Staff, and belonging to Royal Cinque Ports Yacht Club, Dover.
Lent by Dr. J. Collis Browne. 1874.
Note.—The projection of the vessel's bow, or her beak, as it may be called, is built on the watertight compartment system. The object is to obtain more buoyancy forward for the yacht, and to render her a dry ship. Her dimensions are as follows :—Length, deck, 62 feet; beak at bow, 12 feet; total length over all, 74 feet; beam, 16½ feet; depth, 7¼ feet; draft, forward, 1 foot 6 inches; aft, 5 feet 6 inches. Scale of model, ¾ inch to 1 foot.

38. WHOLE MODEL of a proposed iron clad ship of war, with retreating sides, and fore and aft projections, built in watertight compartments. The armour plating to be 3 feet in thickness, and 12 feet in depth. The upper white line on the hull of the Model shows the fighting floatation line of the ship. The lower white line repre-

sents the sea-going line of ship. The ship is proposed to be driven by single or twin screw propulsion. Its system of construction patented in 1872. Scale of model ⅛th of an inch to 1 foot.
    Lent by Dr. J. Collis Browne, 34, Leadenhall Street, E.C.   1874.

39. WHOLE MODEL, rigged, of the Imperial German armour-plated ship of war, "KONIG WILHELM;" designed by Mr. E. J. Reed. Built 1869 by the Thames Iron Works and Shipbuilding Co.
    Note.—The ship's principal dimensions are:—Length, 365 feet; breadth, 60 feet; tons, 6,000; horse-power, 1,150, nominal. Engines by Messrs. Maudslay, Sons, & Field.
    Lent by E. J. Reed, Esq., M.P., C.B.   1874.

40. WHOLE MODEL of the screw steamship "FARADAY;" constructed for Messrs. Siemens Brothers specially for employment in carrying and laying electric telegraph cables for ocean telegraph lines,
    Lent by Dr. C. W. Siemens, Queen Anne's Gate, Westminster.   1874.

41. MODELS of the "Glen" line Company's clipper screw steamships for the China trade. These vessels are employed between London and China direct viâ Suez Canal.
    Lent by Messrs. MacGregor, Gow, & Co., East India Avenue, E.C.   1874.
    Note.—These models represent a fleet of steamers of about the following dimensions:—Length, 330 feet; breadth, 35 feet; depth, 25 feet; tons gross, 2,106; horse power, 330, nominal.

CLASS II.

Half Block Models, of Sailing Ships and Steam Ships, showing Lines and Forms.

50. HALF MODEL of the Peninsular and Oriental Company's screw steamer "DELHI." Tons 1,898, horse-power 400. Makers of the engines, Messrs. Ravenhill, Easton, and Company. Launched September 1863. Built by Messrs. Money Wigram and Sons.

    Lent by the Peninsular and Oriental Steam Navigation Company. 1868.

51. HALF MODEL of the Peninsular and Oriental Company's screw steamer "CHARKIEH." Tons 1,615, horse-power 350. Makers of the engines, Messrs. J. and G. Rennie. Launched December 1864. Built by the Thames Iron Works Company, Limited.

    Lent by the Peninsular and Oriental Steam Navigation Company. 1868.

52. HALF MODEL of the Peninsular and Oriental Company's screw steamer "DAKAHLIEH." Tons 1,553, horse-power 350. Makers of the engines, Messrs. J. and G. Rennie. Launched February 1865. Built by Messrs. Money Wigram and Sons.

    Lent by the Peninsular and Oriental Steam Navigation Company. 1868.

53. HALF MODEL of the Peninsular and Oriental Company's screw steamer "TANJORE." Tons 1,971, horse-power 400. Makers of the engines, Messrs. Ravenhill, Easton, and Company. Launched April 1865. Built by the Thames Iron Works Company, Limited.

    Lent by the Peninsular and Oriental Steam Navigation Company. 1868.

54. HALF MODEL of the Peninsular and Oriental Company's screw steamer "SURAT." Tons 2,578, horse-power 500. Makers of the engines, Messrs. C. A. Day and Company. Launched March 1866. Built by Messrs. C. A. Day and Company, Southampton.

    Lent by the Peninsular and Oriental Steam Navigation Company. 1868.

CLASS II.—HALF BLOCK MODELS.   23

55. HALF MODEL of the Peninsular and Oriental Company's screw steamer "GOLCONDA." Tons 1,909. Horse power 400. Launched 2nd December 1863, by the Thames Iron Works Company. Length (register) 314 ft. 3 in., breadth 38 ft. 3 in., depth 26 ft. 6 in. Engines (Wolf's double cylinder) by Messrs. Humphreys & Tennant.
  Presented by the Peninsular and Oriental Company.   1865.

56. HALF MODEL of the Peninsular and Oriental Company's paddle steamer "NYANZA." Horse power 450. Engines (oscillating) by Mr. H. G. Rennie. Launched 3rd November 1864, by the Thames Iron Works Company. Length (register) 327 ft. 3 in., breadth 36 ft. 2 in., depth 27 ft. 6 in. Tonnage 2,082.
  Presented by the Peninsular and Oriental Company.   1865.

57. SERIES of HALF BLOCK MODELS, presented in 1867 by Messrs. R. Napier & Sons, Glasgow, illustrating the designs for, and interior arrangement of ships of war, on the combined Turret and Broadside system, proposed by the late Admiral E. P. Halsted, R.N. Designed May 1866. See also whole Models, No. 4, Class I., page 11.

 2. Half block Model of proposed ship of war "POWERFUL," classed as a second rate. 6 Turrets.
  Turrets - - - - 6
  Number of guns in turrets - 12
  Length of ship 438 ft. 9 in. Breadth 67 ft. 6 in. Depth 28 ft. Load draught 26 ft. 6 in. Tonnage 9,652, builders' old measurement. Displacement, 13,200 tons.

  Note.—This model is on a mahogany stand, and fitted to blocks. The starboard side shows the ship as completely constructed. The port side gives a longitudinal through section of the ship's internal arrangement.
Designed May 1866. Scale ¼ inch to 1 foot.

 3. Half block Model of proposed ship of war "DAUNTLESS," classed as a third rate. 5 Turrets.
  Turrets - - - - 5
  Number of guns in turrets - 10
  Length of ship 422 ft. 6 in. Breadth 65 feet. Depth 28 feet. Load draught 26 feet 6 inches.

Tonnage 8,618, builders' old measurement. Displacement 12,100 tons.

Designed May 1866. Scale ¼ in. to 1 foot.

Note.—This model hangs at back of case. The starboard side shows the ship completely constructed. The port side gives a longitudinal through section of the ship's internal arrangement.

4. Half block Model of the proposed ship of war "FORMIDABLE," classed as a fourth rate. 4 Turrets.

Turrets - - - - 4
Number of guns in turrets - 8

Length of ship 390 ft. Breadth 60 ft. Depth 26 ft. 6 in. Load draught 25 ft. 6 in. Tonnage 6,778, builders' old measurement. Displacement, 10,000 tons.

Designed May 1866. Scale ¼-inch to 1 foot.

Note.—This model hangs at back of case. The starboard side shows the ship completely constructed. The port side gives a longitudinal through section, showing the ship's internal arrangement.

5. Half block Model of the proposed ship of war "DEFENCE," classed as a fifth rate. 3 Turrets.

Turrets - - - - 3
Number of guns in turrets - - 6

Length of ship 373 ft. 9 in. Breadth 57 ft. 6 in. Depth 26 ft. 6 in. Load draught 25 ft. 6 in. Tonnage 5,906, builders' old measurement. Displacement, 9,100 tons.

Designed May 1866. Scale ¼-inch to 1 foot.

Note.—The model shows starboard side, ship as completely constructed. The port side gives a longitudinal through section, showing the ship's internal arrangement. This model hangs at back of case.

7. Half block Model of the proposed ship of war "VIGILANT," classed as a seventh rate. 2 Turrets.

Turrets - - - - 2
Number of guns in turrets - - 4

Length of ship 346 ft. 3 in. Breadth 52 ft. 6 in. Depth 25 ft. Load draught 24 ft. 6 in. Tonnage 4,615, builders' old measurement. Displacement, 7,400 tons.

Designed May 1866. Scale ¼-inch to 1 foot.

CLASS II.—HALF BLOCK MODELS. 25

Note.—This model hangs at back of case. The starboard side shows ship completely constructed. The port side gives a longitudinal through section, showing the ship's internal arrangement.
See also whole Models, No. 4, Class I., p. 11.

58. HALF BLOCK MODEL of H.M.'s ship "WATERWITCH," built of iron, 2 guns, 160 horse-power. Scale ¼-inch to 1 foot. Length 162 ft., breadth 32 ft., draught of water 10 ft. 10 in. forward, 11 ft. 4 in. aft, tonnage 778. Displacement 1,190 tons, speed 9·255 knots. Area of midship section immersed 344 square feet. Built by contract by the Thames Iron Shipbuilding Company, in the River Thames. Laid down in November 1864; launched in June 1866.
Designed by Rear-Admiral Geo. Elliot and the Controller's Department, Admiralty, to be propelled on the hydraulic principle.
The armament was two 6-ton rifled guns.
The complement of men was 80. 1869.

59. HALF BLOCK MODEL of the screw steamships "MATABAN" and "IRRAWADDY." The British and Burmese Steam Navigation Company. Keel length 340 ft., breadth 36 ft., depth 28 ft. Tons, register, 2,514. Built 1874, by W. Denny and Brothers.
Lent by Messrs. W. Denny and Brothers, Dumbarton.
1874.

60. HALF BLOCK MODEL of screw steamships "VENETIA," "LOMBARDY," "GWALIOR," and "NYZAM." The Peninsular and Oriental Steam Navigation Company. Keel length 350 ft., breadth 38 ft., depth 28 ft. 9 in. Tons 2,513. Built 1873, by W. Denny and Brothers.
Lent by Messrs. W. Denny and Brothers, Dumbarton.
1874.

61. HALF BLOCK MODEL of the screw steamships "CATHAY" and "HYDASPES." African mail ships. Keel length 360 ft., breadth 39 ft., depth 30 ft. 3 in. Tons, o.m. 2,723. Built 1872, by W. Denny and Brothers.
Lent by Messrs. W. Denny and Brothers, Dumbarton.
1874.

62. HALF BLOCK MODEL of the Royal Mail screw steamship "BOYNE." Keel length 358 ft. 6 in., breadth

40 ft. 5 in., depth 34 ft. 6 in. Tons, o.m., 2,882. Built 1871, by W. Denny and Brothers.

The above four Models lent by Messrs. W. Denny and Brothers, Dumbarton. 1874.

63. HALF BLOCK MODEL of the Atlantic screw steamers "NEVADA" and "IDAHO." Liverpool and New York line. Built 1868, for the Liverpool and Great Western Steamship Company, by the Palmer's Shipbuilding Company, Limited. Length 352 ft. ; breadth 43 ft. ; depth 30 ft. Tonnage gross 3,132 ; horse-power 440 nominal ; speed 13 knots per hour. Scale $\frac{1}{60}$ full size.

Lent by the Palmer's Shipbuilding Company, Limited, Newcastle-on-Tyne. 1874.

See also No. 18, Class I., p. 15.

64. HALF-BLOCK MODEL of the steam screw yacht "CORNELIA," built 1868, for Earl Vane, by the Palmer's Shipbuilding Company, Limited. Length 176 ft. ; breadth 20¾ ft. ; depth 14 ft. Tonnage gross 212 ; horse-power 50 nominal ; speed 11 knots per hour. Scale $\frac{1}{48}$th full size.

Lent by the Palmer's Shipbuilding Company Limited, Newcastle-on-Tyne. 1874.

See also No. 16, Class I., p. 14.

65. HALF BLOCK MODEL of clipper ship "FIERY CROSS," built 1855. Length 173 ft. ; breadth 31 ft. 6 in. ; depth 18 ft. 9 in. Tonnage, o.m., 810. Scale ¼-inch to 1 foot.

Lent by Mr. J. Campbell. 1869.

See Model, No. 29, page 18.

66. HALF BLOCK MODEL of a British merchant clipper ship. Length 170 ft. ; beam 28 ft. Scale ¼-inch to 1 foot.

Lent by Mr. J. Campbell. 1869.

67. HALF MODEL showing the external iron riders of H.M.S. "CALEDONIA," iron-cased frigate, built in 1863 at Woolwich.

Lent by Mr. George Turner, late Master Shipwright, Woolwich Dockyard. 1864.

68. HALF MODEL of Messrs. Westwood and Baillie's design for an armour-plated turret ship, showing broadside, and fore and aft angular firing. Tons 6,300. Guns 22. Horse-power 1,160 nominal.

Lent by Messrs. Westwood and Baillie. 1867.

CLASS II.—HALF BLOCK MODELS.

69. HALF MODEL of the iron sailing ship, "VICTORY."
Tons 1,198. Built 1863. Designed and built by Messrs. Laurence Hill and Co.
    Presented by Messrs. Laurence Hill and Co., Glasgow.
                                                                               1865.

70. HALF MODEL of Messrs. Jardine, Mathison, and Co's. paddle steamer "GLENGYLE," constructed for the navigation of the river Yangtzee. Tons 2,040, nominal horse-power 400. Designed and built by W. Denny and Brothers, Dumbarton.
    Presented by Messrs. W. Denny and Brothers, Dumbarton, N.B.   1865.

71. HALF MODEL of a Corvette of the "ALABAMA" class.
    Proposed and lent by Mr. George Turner, late Master Shipwright, Woolwich Dockyard.   1864.

Note.—During the civil war in America, 1860–1864, the American Confederate States celebrated corvette "ALABAMA," built in England, was sunk in an action fought off Cherbourg on 19th June 1864, with the Federal ship-of-war "KERSAGE."

CLASS III.

Models of Construction, Sailing Ships and Steam Ships, Wood and Iron. Keels, Timbers, Frames, Beams, Knees, &c. Sectional Models.

1. MODELS, 5 in number, of ship construction, wood and iron. Purchased 1874.

1. Half midship section of a corvette, on $\frac{1}{2}$-in. scale showing the method of ship's framing, fastening beams to ships' sides, &c. Wood construction.

2. Half midship section of an armour-plated ship of war, on $\frac{1}{2}$-in. scale, showing method of the construction of ship's frame, the armour plating and backing, &c. Iron construction.

3. Model showing the present system of framing armour-plated ships of war in Her Majesty's service, with ship's skin plating attached. Scale 1 in. to 1 ft.

4. Half block model, on a scale of $\frac{1}{4}$ in. to 1 ft., showing the principal lines used in "laying off" the "fore" body of a merchant ship.

5. Half block model, on a scale of $\frac{1}{4}$ in. to 1 ft., showing the principal lines used in "laying off" the "after" body of a merchant ship.

6. Diagram, showing the lines used in "laying off" the "after" body of a screw frigate. Wood construction.

The foregoing five models and diagram, purchased 1874.

Note.—The above models and diagram, illustrating ship construction, are used for reference in the instruction of students in naval architecture. They are prepared under the direction of the Science and Art Department. Similar models form part of the travelling apparatus for instruction in science, lent by the Department to science schools and classes of this country. A few further explanatory remarks as to what the models are intended to represent may be of service.

1. The model of the half-midship section of the wood ship shows the system now in general use in Her Majesty's dockyards of framing with long and short armed floors in alternation with the ordinary

floors and first futtocks, formerly called crosspieces and half-floors. The object of this arrangement is to assist the conversion of the timbers, and to improve the shift of butts; the frames having the long and short armed floors are termed filling frames in contradistinction to the regular frames.

2. The model of the half-midship section of the iron-clad ship shows the longitudinal system of framing, as adopted in Her Majesty's ships "AGINCOURT" "MINOTAUR," and "NORTHUMBERLAND," and also the method of forming and combining the several parts of the hull.

3. The small sectional model represents the mode now adopted in Her Majesty's service of framing iron-clad ships, more particularly of forming and fitting the frame plates, being a modification of that shown by the larger model. The object of this plan is to economise weight of materials and cost of workmanship, and is termed the bracket system of framing.

4-5. The block models are also intended to aid the students in understanding the principles of the geometry of shipbuilding or "laying off;" they show the forms that the several lines assume by the ship, and how she is cut by the different planes.

6. The diagram, as will be seen, represents the after-body of a wood screw ship as laid off. It has not been considered necessary to prepare a similar diagram of the fore-body, as the character of the lines used in "fairing" is nearly identical. See Fore-body in Fincham's Laying off.

2. MODEL of the section of a ship's side.
Lent by Mr. J. Walker. 1867.

3. MODEL of the section of a ship's side, with armour plates attached.
Lent by Mr. J. Walker. 1867.

4. MODEL of part of the frame of a ship of war, as proposed by Mr. Joseph Tucker.
Presented by Mr. J. S. Tucker. 1865.

5. Comparative MODEL, showing the oval stern, with quarter ports for guns on each deck.
Presented by Mr. J. S. Tucker. 1865.

6. TWO MODELS of midship sections of vessels. 1865.
Presented by Mr. J. S. Tucker.

7. MODEL showing a method of total under-side fastenings for deck planking.
Presented by Mr. J. S. Tucker. 1865.

8. MODEL of the midship section of a design for a four-decked ship of war, the "DUKE OF KENT," to carry 170 guns.
> Proposed by Mr. Joseph Tucker in 1809, when Master Shipwright of Plymouth Dockyard.
> Presented by Mr. J. S. Tucker. 1865.
See Drawing, Class XIV., No. 40, page 81.

9. TWO SPECIMENS of patent grooves and metal sheathing for iron ships.
Presented by Mr. T. B. Daft, C.E. 1864.

10. SPECIMEN of zinc sheathing for iron vessels ("Daft's" patent). Patented September 1863.
Presented by Mr. T. B. Daft, C.E. 1865.

11. TWO MODELS illustrating plan of wood sheathing for iron ships. Model (marked H.N. 2) shows finish to wood sheathing.
Proposed by Messrs. Hooper and Nickson, Liverpool.
Lent by Hooper and Nickson, Liverpool. 1870.

12. THREE MODELS (18 × 12 inches) of the after parts of the submerged propeller ships "ARCHIMEDES," built in 1839, and "NOVELTY," built 1839–40.
> Lent by Mr. Henry Wimshurst, the constructor of the original vessels. 1873.

> 1. Model of the after body of the original experimental vessel, "ARCHIMEDES," built 1839, as prepared for the application of the submerged screw propeller by Mr. H. Wimshurst, Limehouse.
> The model has also attached to it, a model in wood of the original screw propeller applied to the ship and used on her first voyage in May 1839.

CLASS III.—CONSTRUCTION. 31

2. Model showing the complete framing and construction of the after body of the second submerged propeller or screw steamship, the "NOVELTY" built by Mr. H. Wimshurst, 1839-40.
This vessel was the first to be fitted with direct-acting engines to drive screw propeller, and having means for shipping or unshipping same.

3. Model of the after body of the "NOVELTY," the second screw steamer, built in 1839-40, showing Mr. H. Wimshurst's altered position for the submerged screw propeller.
The above models lent by Mr. H. Wimshurst. 1873.
See also Drawings No. 73, Class XIV., page 89.

13. THREE WHOLE MODELS, illustrating the "double-ended principle" in shipbuilding; and one sectional MODEL of an "after end," fitted with nautilus propellers, patented by the late Mr. Kennedy, 28th October 1863.
The largest of these models, which was the first made, dates back to March 1862, and was placed in the Museum of Patents in September 1862. The last one placed there was made for the drawings prepared for the patent. The novel points consist in the new form of bottom, propellers, rudders, battery, &c. The propellers are also the subject of a patent, dated May 1862.
Presented by the late Mr. John Kennedy, Whitehaven. 1864.

14. MODEL, midship Section, showing the construction of the combined Turret and Broadside Armour-plated iron ships, proposed by the late Vice-Admiral E. P. Halstead, R.N., in 1866.
Scale ½ in. to 1 ft.
Presented by Messrs. R. Napier & Sons, Glasgow.
1867.

Note.—The system of diagonal trussing for the spar deck is a patent by R. Napier, Esq.
See also Class I., No. 4A, page 11.

15. Series of WHOLE and HALF BLOCK MODELS, in Wood. 59 in number. Illustrating theoretical principles of ships' lines.
Lent by Mr. John Scott Russell, F.R.S. 1868.

Note.—These models illustrate the gradual development of Mr. John Scott Russell's wave-line system for ship construction, and exhibit intermediate steps from the square box model (No. 59) to the complete theoretical rendering of the idea in model No. 1. The different models represent the experimental forms used for instruction and comparison.

The following MODELS, Nos. 3, 5, 8, 12, 13, 14, 17, 18, 20, 21, 22, 24, 34, 35, 36, represent some of the most successful steamers and yachts which have been built upon the wave-line system by Mr. Russell :—

3. Whole Model, complete, of the paddle-wheel steamship " BARON OSY," designed and built by Mr. J. Scott Russell, and running between London and Antwerp as a passenger and cargo vessel, 1874.

5. Whole Model, complete, of a small trading screw steamer.

8. Whole Model, complete, of the Sydney and Melbourne Royal Mail Steam Packet Company's paddle-wheel steamer " PACIFIC." Tons, 1,470. Horse-power, 500. Designed and built by Mr. J. Scott Russell.

See Drawing of Engines, Nos. 48, 49, Class XIV., page 82.

12. Whole Model, complete, of a steam screw collier with long hull.

13. Whole Model, complete, of a trading screw steamer.

14. Whole Model, complete, of a paddle-wheel trading steamer of the " HALDER " class. Built

17. Whole Model, complete, of a steam screw collier lengthened. A similar vessel to the " EAGLE " and " CAROLINE " screw colliers. Built

18. Whole Model, complete, of a long screw steam collier.

20. Whole Model, complete, of the Prussian man-of-war paddle-wheel steamer " DANTZIG," 12 guns, 400 horse-power. Designed and built by Mr. Scott Russell.

21. Whole Model, complete, of the paddle-wheel passenger and trading steamer " ROUEN," running between Newhaven and Dieppe. Owned by

CLASS III.—CONSTRUCTION. 33

London, Brighton, and South Coast Railway Company.
See Model No. 11.

22. Whole Model, complete, of a passenger and trading screw steamer, designed and built by Mr. Scott Russell. The engines and boilers are placed aft. The passenger saloon and cabin accommodation is amidships. Further cabin room, right aft.

24. Whole Model, complete, of the paddle-wheel steam yacht "WAVE QUEEN," designed and built by Mr. J. Scott Russell. This vessel was remarkable for her extreme length, very narrow breadth, and shallow depth, all clearly illustrated by this model. She attained a high rate of speed.
See also Model No. 9.

1. Theoretical Principles. Model, whole block, illustrating solid of least resistance, with elliptical midship section.

2. Whole Model, ribband model, deck retreating. Starboard side built complete. Port side showing ribband.

4. Theoretical Principles. Block Model, whole, illustrating lines of ships, buttocks, and water-lines.

6. Whole Model of a sailing ship. Starboard side planked and complete. Port side shows timbers and waling. Bow portion, the ribband. Wooden ship construction.

7. Whole Model, ribband model. Deck retreating. Wooden ship construction. Port side shows long ribband. Starboard side unfinished.

9. Practical Shipbuilding, block model of the buttock and water-line of the paddle-wheel steam yacht "WAVE QUEEN." See Model No. 24.

10. Whole Model, ribband model. Wooden ship construction. Starboard side completely finished. Port side, ribband.

11. Practical Shipbuilding, block model of the buttock and water-lines of the paddle-wheel steamer "ROUEN." See Model No. 21.

c 2

12. Theoretical Principles. Block Model of ship's lines, buttocks, &c.

15. Block Model. Whole model, showing lines and buttock of a small steam screw yacht.

16. Theoretical Principles. Block Model, whole. Waterline and buttocks.

19. Whole Model of the sailing schooner yacht "AMERICA." Built at New York in 1851. Designed by Mr. Steers, N. Y.

23. Hollow block Model, showing form and water-line of a lengthened steam screw collier.

25. Block Model of the hull and lines of the Prussian gunboats, paddle-wheel steamers, "NIX" and "SALAMANDER," water-line, &c. See Drawing, Nos. 51, 52, Class XIV., page 82.

26. Block Model, whole, showing water-line and form of paddle-wheel steamers built on the lines and model of the "SCHAFFHAUSEN" steamer.

27. Half block Model. Key model for a yacht or small vessel.

28. Half block Model. Key model for a yacht or small vessel.

29. Half block Model. Key model for a yacht or small vessel.

30. Block Model, whole, illustrating lines of ships, buttocks, &c.

31. Block Model, whole, illustrating lines of ships, buttocks, &c.

32. Block Model, whole, of a flat-bottomed shallow boat, for Indian river navigation. Iron construction.

33. Half block Model. Buttock lines.

34. Whole Model, block, of the sailing yacht "UNDINE." Owned by his Grace the Duke of Sutherland.

35. Whole Model, block, of the sailing yacht "THEMIS."

36. Whole Model, block, of the schooner sailing yacht "TITANIA."

37. Whole Model of a sailing cutter yacht Form and water-line.

38. Theoretical Principles. Block Model. Water-lines of a ship.

39. Half block Models. The working model used for the construction of iron ships, giving the sizes and thicknesses of the plates, and other working detail.

40. Half block Models. The working model used in the construction of iron ships, giving the sizes and thicknesses of the plates, and other working detail.

41. Block Model, whole, of a shallow-draught river steamer, for Indian river navigation. Iron construction.

42. Sectional Model, H.M.S. "WARRIOR," built 1860, as originally designed by Mr. Scott Russell, showing proposed method of armour plating, &c.

43. Theoretical Principles. Hollow block Model of a ship's hull, showing form and water-line.

44. Theoretical Principles. Hollow block Model of a ship's hull, showing form for least resistance, water-line, &c.

45. Theoretical Principles. Hollow block Model of a ship's hull, showing form and water-line.

46. Theoretical Principles. Hollow block Model of a steamer's hull, showing form and water-line.

47. Theoretical Principles. Hollow block Model of a ship's hull, old form, showing form and water-line.

48. Hollow block Model of the hull and water-line of the Royal Mail screw steamer "VICTORIA and ADELAIDE," Australian liner. Designed by Mr. J. Scott Russell.

49. Theoretical Principles. Hollow block Model of a long ship's hull, showing form and water-line.

50. Theoretical Principles. Hollow block Model of the hull of a paddle-wheel steamship with retreating sides for the wheel space.

51. Theoretical Principles. Hollow block Model of a steamship's hull. Lines and form on the wave-line principle.

52. Theoretical Principles. Hollow block Model of a ship's hull, old form.

53. Theoretical Principles. Hollow block Model of a ship's hull on the lines of a Dutch galiot.

54. Theoretical Principles. Hollow block Model of a long ship's hull, showing form and water-line.

55. Theoretical Principles. Hollow block Model, illustrating " wave-line" square sections of a ship's hull.

56. Theoretical Principles. Hollow block Model of a ship's hull, old form.

57. Whole block Model, showing form and water-line of a ship of war, designed by Mr. Scott Russell.

58. Whole block Model, showing form and water-line of a proposed ship of war, designed by Mr. Scott Russell.

59. Theoretical Principles. Hollow block Model. Square block form of a hull and water-line.

The foregoing 59 models, illustrating theoretical and practical principles of ship construction, lent by Mr. J. Scott Russell, F.R.S. 1868.
See also Engravings, Class XIV., No. 65, page 83.

16. HALF MODEL, showing a proposal for double bulkheads in iron ships capable of holding water in case of fire; for strength and security to ship and cargo; and affording a simple means of testing the tightness of the bulkhead itself. Proposed by Dr. John Taylor, M.D., late Professor of Natural Philosophy in the Andersonian University, Glasgow.
Presented by Dr. John Taylor, M.D. 1873.

17. MODEL illustrating McCool's designs and methods for stopping holes in ships' bottoms by means of galvanized iron plates and screw bars.
Lent by Mr. J. McCool. 1872.

18. MODEL, designed to illustrate the fore turret and fore deck arrangement, in the proposed combined turret and broadside ships of war, designed by the late Vice-Admiral E. P. Halsted, R.N., in 1866.
Note.—This model shows proposed method for carrying spar deck, and clearing fore part of ship of

CLASS III.—CONSTRUCTION.   37

hamper, so as to obtain a thorough end on line of fire.
>Presented by Messrs. R. Napier & Sons, Glasgow.   1867.
See also Class I., No. 4A, page 11.

19. MODEL of two half sterns of a first-rate ship of war, wood construction, showing "Blake's" method for the framing of the timber, &c., and gallery. Designed by Mr. R. Blake, Master Shipwright in H.M.'s Dockyards, 1806–1855.
>Presented by the Rev. J. Hardie, Falmouth. 1866.

20. MODEL of "Blake's" plan for the prevention of water entering a ship, in the event of any accident to the screw. Designed by Mr. R. Blake, Master Shipwright in H.M.'s Dockyards, 1806–1855.
>Presented by the Rev. J. Hardie, Falmouth. 1866.

21. MODEL of "Blake's" plan for connecting beams to ship's side. Designed by Mr. R. Blake, Master Shipwright in H.M.'s Dockyards, 1806–1855.
>Presented by the Rev. J. Hardie, Falmouth. 1866.

22. MODEL on "Blake's" plan of futtock timbers, fitted with side chock. Designed by Mr. R. Blake, Master Shipwright in H.M.'s Dockyards, 1806–1855.
>Presented by the Rev. J. Hardie, Falmouth. 1866.

23. MODEL on "Blake's" plan of futtock timber with side scarf. Designed by Mr. R. Blake, Master Shipwright in H.M.'s Dockyards, 1806–1855.
>Presented by the Rev. J. Hardie, Falmouth. 1866.

24. MODEL on "Blake's" plan of futtock to dispense with angle chock. Designed by Mr. R. Blake, Master Shipwright in H.M.'s Dockyards, 1806–1855.
>Presented by the Rev. J. Hardie, Falmouth. 1866.

25. MODEL on "Blake's" plan of two floors made good with chocks at the side of keel. Designed by Mr. R. Blake, Master Shipwright in H.M.'s Dockyards, 1806–1855.
>Presented by the Rev. J. Hardie, Falmouth. 1866.

26. MODEL of floor and first buttock united together on the old plan. Designed by Mr. R. Blake, Master Shipwright in H.M.'s Dockyards, 1806–1855.
>Presented by the Rev. J. Hardie, Falmouth. 1866.

27. MODEL of common floor timber, chocked at the heel on the side of keel. Designed by Mr. R. Blake, Master Shipwright in H.M.'s Dockyards, 1806–1855.
 Presented by the Rev. J. Hardie, Falmouth. 1866.

28. MODEL on "Blake's" plan of two bent floor timbers with saw-kerf in middle of moulding side, to assist the bending. Designed by Mr. R. Blake, Master Shipwright in H.M.'s Dockyards, 1806–1855.
 Presented by the Rev. J. Hardie, Falmouth. 1866.

29. HALF BLOCK MODEL. Stern elevation of a three-deck line-of-battle ship. Wood construction. Starboard side, showing possible disposition of guns so as to obtain a nearly all-round and a right-aft line of fire.
Designed by Mr. R. Blake, Master Shipwright, H.M.'s Dockyards, 1806–1855.
 Presented by Rev. J. Hardie, Falmouth. 1866.

30. WHOLE MODEL. Stern elevation of a three-deck line-of-battle ship. Wood construction.
Starboard side shows stern elevation completed.
Port side shows disposition of ship's timbers, wales, &c., and emplacement of gun ports for a right-aft and nearly all-round fire.
Designed by Mr. R. Blake, Master Shipwright, H.M.'s Dockyards, 1806–1855.
 Presented by Rev. J. Hardie, Falmouth. 1866.

31. HALF BLOCK MODEL. Stern elevation of a three-deck line-of-battle ship. Wood construction. Starboard side, showing wales and plan of vertical timbering.
Mr. R. Blake, Master Shipwright, H.M.'s Dockyard, 1806–1855
 Presented by Rev. J. Hardie, Falmouth. 1866.

32. HALF BLOCK MODEL. Stern elevation of a three-deck line-of-battle ship. Wood construction.
Starboard side showing wales, side timbering, and proposed stern disposition of timbers, ports, &c.
Designed by Mr. R. Blake, Master Shipwright, H.M.'s Dockyards, 1806–1855.
 Presented by Rev. J. Hardie, Falmouth. 1866.

33. WHOLE MODEL of the bow of a frigate. Wood construction.

CLASS III.—CONSTRUCTION. 39

The upper portion of the model shows the bow of ship completed; the lower part shows disposition and arrangement of timbers.
Starboard side on an old form; port side on improved form of bow.
Designed by Mr. R. Blake, Master Shipwright, H.M.'s Dockyards, 1806-1855.
Presented by Rev. J. Hardie, Falmouth.   1866.

34. HALF BLOCK MODEL of the starboard bow of a three-deck line-of-battle ship, about 1835-1840. Wood construction, showing possible line of bow fire from four guns.
Mr. R. Blake, Master Shipwright, H.M.'s Dockyards, 1806-1855.
Presented by Rev. J. Hardie, Falmouth.   1866.

35. HALF BLOCK MODEL of the port bow of a three-deck line-of-battle ship. Wood construction. About 1840-1850, showing disposition so as to obtain a possible bow line of fire from six guns.
Designed by Mr. R. Blake, Master Shipwright, H.M.'s Dockyards, 1806-1855.
Presented by Rev. J. Hardie, Falmouth.   1866.

36. MODEL of an upper deck gun port, showing disposition of framing and timbers.
Designed by Mr. R. Blake, Master Shipwright, H.M.'s Dockyards, 1806-1855.
Presented by Rev. J. Hardie, Falmouth.   1866.

37. FIVE PIECES, Models, illustrating floor timbers for wooden ships.
Proposed by Mr. R. Blake, Master Shipwright, H.M.'s Dockyards, 1806-1855.
Presented by Rev. J. Hardie, Falmouth.   1866.

38. MODEL of the side of a ship of war, wood construction, showing side of lower deck port, and proposed method of re-sheathing an old ship below the water-line.
Proposed by Mr. R. Blake, Master Shipwright, H.M.'s Dockyards, 1806-1855.
Presented by Rev. J. Hardie, Falmouth.   1866.

39. THREE PIECES, Keel Blocks, Models.
Proposed by Mr. R. Blake, Master Shipwright, H.M.'s. Dockyards, 1806-1855.
Presented by Rev. J. Hardie, Falmouth.   1866.

40. MODEL. Design for an improved head board for ships of war. Wood construction.
Proposed by Mr. R. Blake, Master Shipwright, H.M.'s Dockyards, 1806–1855.
Presented by Rev. J. Hardie, Falmouth.   1866.

41. EIGHT MODELS, illustrating various methods, old forms, and new proposals, for connecting beams to ships' sides. Wood construction.
Designed by Mr. R. Blake, Master Shipwright, H.M.'s Dockyards, 1806–1855.
Presented by Rev. J. Hardie, Falmouth.   1866.

42. WHOLE MODEL of a proposed and patented method for steam ship construction, designed by Dr. J. Collis Browne, late army medical staff.
Note.—The ship is designed with a view of obtaining extraordinary buoyancy, increased speed and safety, freedom from pitching and scending. She is dry in the heaviest weather, and is a safety ship.
The Model is fitted with a working screw propeller designed by Dr. J. Collis Browne, which is driven by model inverted screw engines, and copper boiler.
Lent by Dr. J. Collis Browne.   1874.

43. WHOLE MODEL of a proposed screw steamship of new design by Captain Archibald Thompson, Liverpool.
The ship has channel ways on each side of the keel, running deep aft, and to nothing forward.
They form a water lead to the screw, which is placed forward well under ship's counter.
Lent by Mr. A. Thompson.   1874.

44. The contractor's MODEL actually used for the construction of the "GREAT EASTERN" steamship, showing size and fittings, &c., of the Exterior iron plating.
Designed by Mr. I. K. Brunel, F.R.S.
Built by J. Scott Russell, F.R.S. This ship was designed in 1852, laid down in 1853, built 1857.
Lent by Mr. John Scott Russell, F.R.S.   1869.

45. The contractor's MODEL actually used for the construction of the "GREAT EASTERN" steamship, showing size and fittings, &c., of the Interior iron plating.
Lent by Mr. John Scott Russell, F.R.S.   1869.

46. MODEL of the construction of the stern of the "GREAT EASTERN" steamship.
Lent by Mr. John Scott Russell, F.R.S.   1869.

CLASS IV.

Models of Fitments—Cabins and their fittings. Ports, Skylights, Hatchways, Ladders, &c.—Ventilation of Ships—Fire-hearths and Stoves.

1. MODEL of "Blake's" method for ventilating troop-ships.
Designed by Mr. R. Blake, Master Shipwright in H.M.'s Dockyards, 1806-1855.
Presented by the Rev. J. Hardie, Falmouth. 1866.

2. MODEL of "Blake's" plan for barring in the ports, and showing method of ventilation.
Designed by Mr. R. Blake, Master Shipwright in H.M.'s Dockyards, 1806-1855.
Presented by the Rev. J. Hardie, Falmouth. 1866.

3. "BLAKE'S" improved stopper bolt.
Designed by Mr. R. Blake, Master Shipwright in H.M.'s Dockyards, 1806-1866.
Presented by the Rev. J. Hardie, Falmouth. 1866.

4. SECTIONAL MODEL of a ship's side, showing proposed arrangement 'tween decks for the transport of troops. The model represents accommodation for about 20 men.
Designed by Mr. R. Blake, Master Shipwright, H.M.'s Dockyards, 1806-1855.
Presented by Rev. J. Hardie, Falmouth. 1866.

5. MODEL. Original design for horse stalls, as fitted at Malta, to the ships that conveyed the troops to the Crimea, 1854.
Lent by Mr. W. Ladd, Deptford Dockyard. 1864.

6. FIRE-HEARTHS or ships' cooking stoves. Five Models, illustrating various plans for and arrangement of the above apparatus. Designed and fitted up in H.M.'s ships, royal yachts, &c., by Benham and Sons.
Lent by Messrs. Benham and Sons. 1869.

1. MODEL of ship's fire-hearth or cooking apparatus, 1-8th full size, fitted to H.M.'s Indian relief, steam screw troop-ships, by Benham and Sons. The hearth will cook and bake bread for 1,400 men.

2. MODEL of ship's fire-hearth or cooking apparatus fitted to ships of H.M.'s Navy and troop transport service. "Officers" fire-hearth, will cook and bake for 100 officers.

3. MODEL of circular ship's fire-hearth or cooking apparatus in a circular form, as fitted to the steamships of the Royal Mail West India Company. This hearth will cook and bake bread for 300 passengers.

4. MODEL of a ship's fire-hearth or cooking apparatus fitted to the steamships of the Peninsular and Oriental Company and of the Royal Mail West India Company. Ships' crews hearth, will cook and bake bread for 100 men.

5. MODEL of a ship's fire-hearth or cooking apparatus, fitted on board the steamships of the Peninsular and Oriental Company. The hearth will cook and bake bread for 200 passengers.

The above five models, lent by Messrs. Benham and Sons, Wigmore Street. 1869.

7. PATENT FIRE-HEARTH or cooking stove for yachts.
Lent by Messrs. Pascall Atkey, & Son, Cowes. 1874.

8. ORNAMENTAL STOVE for yacht's saloons and cabins.
Lent by Messrs. Pascall Atkey, & Son. 1874.

Note.—The cooking apparatus and cabin stove for yachts exhibited by Atkey and Son are used on board vessels belonging to the various yacht clubs of Great Britain. The cooking stove, 2 feet 2 inches long by 13 inches wide, will bake, boil, steam, stew, and roast, has a copper boiler for hot water, and plate and dish warmers.

CLASS V.

Appliances used in Ships. Capstans and Windlasses. Tanks, Pumps, &c. Anchors and Chain Cables, and gear connected with them.

---

1. THREE COMPRESSORS for chain cables. *a.* Original; *b.* As proposed by the Surveyor of the Navy, Sir William Symonds; *c.* As proposed by the Plymouth-yard Officers. 1835. 1864.

2. DROGUE. A canvass floating anchor about 2 feet square, used by fishing and other boats, to keep under weigh and head to sea.
Presented by Mr. C. W. Merrifield. 1869.

3. MODEL of "Blake's" slip hook for mooring chains. Designed by Mr. R. Blake, Master Shipwright in H.M.'s Dockyards, 1806-1855.
Presented by the Rev. J. Hardie, Falmouth. 1866.

4. MODEL showing "Blake's" stoppers for letting go anchors. Designed by Mr. R. Blake, Master Shipwright in H.M.'s Dockyards, 1806-1855.
Presented by the Rev. J. Hardie, Falmouth. 1866.

5. MODEL, snatch block, standard or pendant, for hauling in deep-sea lead lines. Designed by Mr. R. Blake, Master Shipwright, H.M.'s Dockyards, 1806-1855.
Presented by Rev. J. Hardie, Falmouth. 1866.

6. MODEL, wood, illustrating part of a proposed toggle. Designed by Mr. R. Blake, Master Shipwright, H.M.'s Dockyards, 1806-1855.
Presented by Rev. J. Hardie, Falmouth. 1866.

7. MODEL of a ship's bulwark, showing an improved method for stowing life buoys between the bulwark stanchions, along ship's side. Designed by Mr. H. S. Harland, Brompton, Scarborough.
Presented. 1874.

8. MODEL of the bows of an armour-plated ship-of-war, illustrating Martin's patent self-canting anchors; their housing in board; and Martin's patent zig-zag chain cable for same.
Lent by Mr. C. Martin, 73, King William Street. 1874.

CLASS VI.
Masts. Rigging, standing and running. Sails.

1. MODEL of the Masts, Rigging, and Sails, of H.M.S. " GANGES," 84 guns. (On a ⅛-in. scale). Length 196 ft. 5¼ in., breadth 52 ft. 2¼ in., tonnage 2,285. Laid down at Bombay in 1819, launched in 1821. Designed as " CANOPUS."
Presented by the late Captain Hugh Talbot Burgoyne. R.N. 1865.

2. MODEL of section of a vessel with masts and sails on the flat-surface principle.
Presented by Lieut. W. Congalton, R.N.R. 1865.

3. Two MODELS of vessels illustrating a new method of rigging ships with flat-surface sails.
Proposed and lent by Lieut. W. Congalton, R.N.R. 1865.

Note.—*a.* Model illustrating a merchant sailing ship, full rigged, of about 1,300 tons burthen. Rigged to show masts and flat surface sails on Lieutenant Congalton's plan.

b. Model illustrating the rig for a screw steamship, " Chinese fashion," with flat surface sails on Lieutenant Congalton's plan.

4. MODEL of Cunningham's self-reefing topsail, or plan for reefing from the deck. Invented by Henry D. P. Cunningham, 1850.
Lent by Mr. H. D. P. Cunningham. 1866.

5. MODEL, working of sails. The upper deck of a ship, showing two different arrangements of Cunningham's patent method for reefing topsails from the deck. The fore-topsail and yard in the model is Cunningham's latest plan and arrangement, 1870. The main topsail and yard is the original plan of Mr. Cunningham, 1850.
Lent by Mr. H. D. P. Cunningham. 1871.

6. MODEL (same model as preceding) working of yards. The upper deck of a ship of three masts, fitted with Cunningham's patent chain gear and windlass, for hauling upon the braces of the lower yards, so as to square or brace them by one operation.
Lent by Mr. H. D. P. Cunningham. 1871.

MASTS.

7. THREE MODELS of Faggot-built MASTS, for line-of-battle ships.
Presented by Mr. J. S. Tucker. 1865.

8. MODEL of a patent Topmast, designed by Captain Turnbull.
Presented by Messrs. Laurence Hill & Co., Glasgow.
1865.

9. MODEL. 4 pieces, painted; illustrating in wood Mr. R. Blake's plans for the construction and building up of the Masts of a ship of war, and showing dispositions of cheeks and outside pieces. Proposed by Mr. R. Blake, Master Shipwright H.M.'s Dockyards, 1806-1855.
Presented by Rev. J. Hardie, Falmouth. 1866.

FITTINGS.

10. MODEL of "Blake's" single hook for futtock shrouds. Designed by Mr. R. Blake, Master Shipwright in H.M.'s Dockyards, 1806-1855.
Presented by the Rev. J. Hardie, Falmouth. 1866.

11. TWO MODELS (*a* and *b*) of "Blake's" patent fids, and plans for fidding topmasts. Designed by Mr. R. Blake, Master Shipwright in H.M.'s Dockyards, 1806-1855.
Presented by the Rev. J. Hardie, Falmouth. 1866.

Note.—One of these models (*b*) shows the fid plan adopted for the Royal Navy after trial on board H.M.S. "QUEEN," "S. VINCENT," "ILLUSTRIOUS," "WARSPITE," "VINDICTIVE," and others. 1807-1813.

12. MODEL of "Blake's" stoppers and fid for shortening the bowsprit. Designed by Mr. R. Blake, Master Shipwright in H.M.'s Dockyards, 1806-1855.
Presented by the Rev. J. Hardie, Falmouth. 1866.

13. MODEL of "Blake's" tumbler hook for letting go the sheet of a boat's sail in cases of emergency. Designed by Mr. R. Blake, Master Shipwright in H.M.'s Dockyards, 1806-1855.
Presented by the Rev. J. Hardie, Falmouth. 1866.

14. Two Models, one iron and one wood, for steps of lower masts, on "Blake's" plan. Designed by Mr. R. Blake, Master Shipwright in H.M.'s Dockyards, 1806–1855.
Presented by the Rev. J. Hardie, Falmouth. 1866.

15. Model of "Blake's" plan, showing alteration in method of Securing Shrouds, and doing away with lower Deadeyes. Designed by Mr. R. Blake, Master Shipwright in H.M.'s Dockyards, 1806–1855.
Presented by the Rev. J. Hardie, Falmouth. 1866.

16. "Blake's" proposed Deadeyes for all ships. Designed by Mr. R. Blake, Master Shipwright in H.M.'s Dockyards, 1806–1855.
Presented by the Rev. J. Hardie, Falmouth. 1866.

17. Five plans (on "Blake's" principle) for Toggles. Designed by Mr. R. Blake, Master Shipwright in H.M.'s Dockyards, 1806–1855.
Presented by the Rev. J. Hardie, Falmouth. 1866.

18. Screw-eye Bolt (on "Blake's" plan). Designed by Mr. R. Blake, Master Shipwright in H.M.'s Dockyards, 1806–1855.
Presented by the Rev. J. Hardie, Falmouth. 1866.

19. Model in iron of a ratchet and lever for setting up ship's shrouds. Designed by Mr. R. Blake, Master Shipwright, H.M.'s dockyards, 1806–1855.
Presented by Rev. J. Hardie, Falmouth. 1866.

Blocks.

20. (*a*.) One common Block, with hemp strop; (*b*) one with iron sheave, and seasoned wire strop, by Mr. Andrew Smith; (*c*) one iron bound block. C. 1864.

21. Common single Block. C. 1864.

22. Two common unfinished Blocks. C. 1864.

23. Two cheek Blocks. C. 1864.

24. Bound Block, with two side hooks. C. 1864.

25. Arnett and Co.'s patent roller Sheave, for ship's blocks. C. 1864.

Rope.

26. Specimen of Hemp Rope. 1864.

27. Specimens of Hempen and Fibrous Rope for ships' rigging, tackle, and cordage.
Lent by Messrs. Frost, Brothers, Ropemakers, London Street, E.C. 1874.

28. Specimens of galvanized Iron wire and Rope, with hearts for the same. 1864.

29. Specimens of Iron wire Rope, for standing rigging. 1864.

30. Specimens of Iron wire rope. 1864.

31. Specimens of Iron wire and Copper wire Rope for ships' rigging, lightning conductors, &c.
Lent by Messrs. Newall & Co., London and Gateshead. 1874.

CLASS VII.

Methods of Propulsion.—Oars and Sculls. Sweeps. Steam Engines, Boilers, Screw propellers, Paddle wheels, &c.

MARINE STEAM ENGINES.

1. PROPELLER for shallow water. Two horizontal oscillating steam cylinders put a crank shaft, lying across the hull, in motion. The crank shaft is three-throw, that is to say, it has a crank at each end and one in the centre. This central crank carries a strong connecting rod, which puts a piston in motion within a third or vacuum cylinder, which is employed to equalize the work done throughout any revolution. To the centre of the length of the connecting rod, or thereabouts, a really simple but apparently complex apparatus is fitted, which gives an oar-like motion to disc propellers, one at either side of the ship.

Designed and lent by Mr. John Garrod White, Ipswich. 1864.

2. MODEL, on a scale of 1 inch to 1 foot, of the horizontal condensing screw engines of H. M.'s turret ship, "PRINCE ALBERT," 2,529 tons. Built 1864. 500 horse-power, nominal.

Lent by Messrs. Humphrys and Tennant, Engineers, Deptford. 1869.

3. MODEL, on a scale of 1½ inches to 1 foot, of the horizontal condensing screw engines of H.M.'s turret ship "MONARCH," 8,164 tons. Built 1868. 1,100 horse-power, nominal.

Lent by Messrs. Humphrys and Tennant, Engineers, Deptford. 1869.

4. MODEL, on a $\frac{1}{10}$th scale, of the horizontal condensing screw engines of H.M.'s ships, "NELSON," built 1814, altered 1860; "CONQUEROR," built 1833, altered 1859; "TAMAR," built 1863. 500 horse-power, nominal. Diameter of cylinders 71 inches. Stroke 3 feet.

Lent by Messrs. Ravenhill, Easton, & Co., Engineers, Ratcliffe, E. 1869.

CLASS VII.—PROPULSION. 49

5. MODEL of the engines of the paddle-wheel steamer "HELEN MCGREGOR" of Liverpool. Designed and arranged in 1843 by G. Forrester & Co., Engineers.
Lent by Messrs. G. Forrester & Co., Liverpool. 1869.
Note.—This engine has two inverted steam cylinders, a very long stroke, and occupies very little hull space. It is a condensing low-pressure engine, and is said to be still at work, 1873.

6. MODEL, on a scale of 1½ inch to a foot, of the oscillating cylinder, paddle-wheel condensing engines of the Holyhead and Kingstown Royal Irish mail steamer "LEINSTER," 750 horse-power nominal. Diameter of cylinders 98 inches, stroke 6 ft. 6 inches.

To the engines are attached, on the same scale, the feathering float Paddle-wheels of the ship, the speed of which is about 21 statute miles per hour.
Lent by Messrs. Ravenhill, Easton, & Co., Engineers.
1869.
See Model of "CONNAUGHT" steamer, No. 24, Class I., p. 17.

7. MODEL of a paddle marine engine, designed by J. Scott Russell, F.R.S., having three oscillating cylinders all connected to one crank on the paddle shaft. One of the cylinders is vertical, the other two are inclined inwards at about 45°.
Lent by Mr. J. Scott Russell, F.R.S. 1869.
The model made by Jabez James, Lambeth.

8. MODEL, working, on a 3 inch to 1 foot scale, of the vertical screw engines of steamship "A. LOPEZ," Cadiz and Havannah Spanish mail service.

The engines are constructed on the hammer or inverted cylinder principle, and have condensers, air and feed pumps, variable expansion gear, &c. The model is a complete working condensing screw engine of about 20 horse-power. It was made in 1866–67, and exhibited in motion at the Paris Universal Exhibition of 1867.
Messrs. W. Denny & Brothers, Engineers and Shipbuilders, Dumbarton. Purchased 1871.

9. SCREW ENGINES. Pair of high-pressure non-condensing screw engines of 20 horse-power, for screw steam yachts, constructed on the hammer or inverted cylinder principle.

Lent by Messrs. Verey & Lange, Engineers, Dover.
1874.
See also Drawing of Messenger's patent steam boiler for yachts and launches, No. 15, p. 50.

10. SCREW ENGINE, full size steam engine for screw launches, or river pleasure yachts. Horse power.
Lent by Messrs. Plenty & Sons, Newbury. 1874.

11. PHOTOGRAPH, of Hardingham's patent three cylinder high-pressure horizontal steam engine, adopted for river screw pleasure yacht propulsion. The engine was designed and patented by Messrs. Brotherhood & Hardingham, Engineers, in 1872-73.
Presented by Messrs. Brotherhood & Hardingham, Engineers, London. 1874.

BOILERS.

12. MODEL in wood, made in parts to take to pieces and show interior disposition. Marine multi-flue steam Boiler, Hawthorn's patent, 1868. Designed for high-pressure working, and with several new and special features, high furnaces, interior water tubes, high steam room.
Lent by R. & W. Hawthorn, Engineers, Newcastle.
1869.

13. MODEL of a set of patent high-pressure Marine steam Boilers.
The boilers are designed for superheating the steam, heating the feed water, and having improved furnaces. Gray's patent.
Lent by Mr. Wm. Gray, Dawlish. 1874.

14. DRAWING, coloured, of a patented multi-flue Marine Boiler, by Messrs. R. & W. Hawthorn, 1868.
See Model of boiler, No. 12.
Lent by Messrs. R. & W. Hawthorn, Newcastle-on-Tyne. 1869.

15. DRAWING of Messenger's patent vertical water-tube Boiler for steam yachts and launches. Designed by Mr. Thomas Messenger, about 1869.
Lent by the makers, Messrs. Verey & Lange, Engineers, Dover. 1874.
See also Screw-engines, No. 9., p. 49.

CLASS VII.—PROPULSION. 51

16. DRAWING of Plenty & Sons' patent horizontal high-pressure steam Boiler, for screw launches or pleasure yachts.
Lent by Messrs. Plenty & Sons, Newbury. 1874.

17. DRAWING. Sections of Gray's patent high-pressure marine steam Boilers showing arrangement of the tubes, steam superheater, water heater, and flues.
Lent by Mr. W. Gray, Dawlish. 1874.
See also Model, No. 13, p. 50.

18. PHOTOGRAPH of a steam Donkey Engine and pump for feeding steam boilers with water. The pumps are single and double acting.
Presented by the makers, Messrs. Brotherhood & Hardingham, Engineers, Compton Street, E.C. 1874.

19. STEAM DONKEY ENGINE and pump, single acting for feeding steam boilers with water.
Lent by makers, Messrs. Alexander Wilson & Co., Engineers, Vauxhall. 1871.

PROPELLERS.

20. THREE MODELS, showing the original design of the after bodies of the first screw steamers "ARCHIMEDES," built 1839; and "NOVELTY," built 1839–40.
The models show the forms of the original submerged screw propellers as fitted to the two ships, and modifications. The "NOVELTY" ultimately was driven by direct-acting engines and a two-bladed screw.
Also see Class III. No. 12, p. 30.
Lent by Mr. H. Wimshurst, Anerley. 1873.

21. MODEL No. 1, of a self-feathering screw propeller adapted for auxiliary and small screw vessels, designed to obviate the necessity of raising the screw when under sail.
Proposed by the inventor and maker, Rev. P. A. Fothergill, Southend. Lent 1871.

22. MODEL No. 2, of Fothergill's self-feathering screw propeller, adapted for auxiliary and small screw vessels, and obviating the necessity of raising the screw when under sail. The screw is entirely self-acting, requires no internal gearing. It can be set to any pitch, and used with any number of blades. See preceding Model.
Inventor and maker, Rev. P. A. Fothergill, Southend.
Lent, 1871.

23. MODEL of a double boat, fitted with a screw-propeller forward, to be driven by manual power; tried in Sussex river Ouse, 1823. The boat only attained a small rate of speed.
Lent by Mr. Burwood Godlee. 1872.

24. MODEL (unfinished) of ship construction, showing a peculiarly made propeller with three fans, also the plan for securing the same. 1846. 1864.

25. WHOLE MODEL of steamboat "JAMES LOWE," fitted in 1838 with a screw propeller, under a patent granted to late Mr. James Lowe in March 1838, for "submerged propellers."

Note.—About the same time a large boat called the "WIZARD" was fitted with a screw or submerged propeller, under the late Mr. J. Lowe's patent.
Presented by Mrs. Henrietta Vansittart. 1874.

26. WHOLE MODEL of the steamship "GREAT BRITAIN," fitted on the late Mr. James Lowe's plan for submerged or screw propellers, a patent for which was granted in March 1838.
Presented by Mrs. Henrietta Vansittart. 1874.

27. MODEL of the stern of a ship, fitted in March 1838 with a screw propeller having one or more curved blades, sections or portions of a screw of uniform or increasing pitch, and placed below the water line of the ship.
Presented by Mrs. Henrietta Vansittart. 1874.

28. MODEL, in wood, of the first shaft and boss made for screw propellers, by late Mr. James Lowe, 1838.
Presented by Mrs. Henrietta Vansittart. 1874.

29. MODEL, in wood, of the first oval boss for screw propellers, made by Mr. James Lowe, 1855.
Presented by Mrs. Henrietta Vansittart. 1874.

30. MODEL, in wood, of the first spherical boss for screw propellers, made by Mr. James Lowe, 1852.
Presented by Mrs. Henrietta Vansittart. 1874.

31. MODEL, in gun metal, of a screw propeller on the late Mr. James Lowe's principle for the blades, 1838.
Presented by Mrs. Henrietta Vansittart. 1874.

CLASS VII.—PROPULSION.

32. MODEL, in wood, on ¼-inch scale, of the "Lowe-Vansittart" screw propeller blades, as invented, and fitted in 1869 by Mrs. Henrietta Vansittart, for trial on board H.M.S. "DRUID," 350 horse power.
Presented by Mrs. Henrietta Vansittart. 1874.

33. DIAGRAM showing the original designs for submerged propellers and their blades, dated "Lowe's steamship propellers," patented 24 March, 1838, by James Lowe. This diagram shows various proposals for the forms of blades of screw propellers.
Presented by Mrs. Henrietta Vansittart. 1874.

34. DIAGRAM illustrating Mr. James Lowe's proposals in 1855 for dividing the blades of screw propellers, and placing them in pairs or sets diagonally across the screw boss. Tried on board H.M.S. "BULLFINCH" in 1857.
Presented by Mrs. Henrietta Vansittart. 1874.

35. ¡DIAGRAM of the modifications proposed in the "Wyche-Lowe" propeller blades, designed in 1852 by the late Mr. James Lowe, and tried on board the S.S. "MISKIN" and "ARGUS." Also the "Lowe-Harris" propeller. 1862.
Presented by Mrs. Henrietta Vansittart. 1874.

36. DIAGRAM of Mr. J. Lowe's fourth improvement in screw propellers in 1862.
Presented by Mrs. Henrietta Vansittart. 1874.

37. DIAGRAM of a screw propeller, and its blades designed by Mrs. Henrietta Vansittart in 1868. Tried on board the Allan-line S.S. "SCANDANAVIAN," 400 horse power, in 1873, and H.M.S. "CADMUS," 21 guns, 400 horse power, in 1869. Known as the "Lowe-Vansittart" screw propeller.
Presented by Mrs. Henrietta Vansittart. 1874.

38. MODEL (full size) of a screw propeller patented by Dr. J. Collis Browne, late Army Medical Staff.
Note.—The propeller is said to possess the following features :—
    a. Absence of vibration.
    b. Reduction of wear and tear in the driving machinery.
    c. Adaptability to any screw steamship.
    d. Facility for checking ships' way ; and for going full speed astern or ahead with increased speed and celerity.

e. Direct action of the water on the axial line of screw.
f. Affording increased steering power.
The steam screw river yacht "LAPWING," owner Dr. J. Collis Browne, is fitted with this screw, and on trial has given successful results.
Lent by Dr. J. Collis Browne, 34, Leadenhall Street, E.C. 1874.

39. BOILER PLATE two specimens, bent and broken, to show the quality of the iron.—(A.) Atlas iron plate, (B.) best iron plate for boilers.
From the Atlas Steel and Iron Works, Sheffield. 1864.

STEAM ENGINE AND BOILER ACCESSORIES.

40. Objects lent by Messrs. Schäffer & Budenberg, 6, King William Street. 1874.
1. 5-inch Pearson's patent lubricator.
2. Mercury vacuum gauge.
3. Thermometer.
4. Bourdon's patent pressure gauges. Steam and vacuum.
5. Schaeffer's patent pressure gauges. Steam and vacuum, with diaphragm springs.
6. Counter, 7 figure, with resetting key. For counting revolutions of engines, &c.

41. SALINOMETER, How's Patent, for measuring the quantity of sea salt in marine steam boilers.
Lent and made by Mr. T. O. Buss, Hatton Garden.
1874.

Note.—In using the Salinometer the water drawn from the boiler should be at 200° Fahrenheit; the instrument is adjusted for this temperature.—It is graduated from 0· to 4·32. 0′ Fresh water. 1·32 sea water, which contains 1 lb. of salt to 32 lb. of water. 2·32 indicates 2 lb. of salt to 32 lb. of water; and so on.
To keep a marine boiler clean, the water should not contain more than 2 lb. salt to 32 lb. water.

CLASS VIII.

Steering Apparatus. Rudders, permanent and temporary. Steering gear of all kinds, Manual and Steam.

1. MODEL of R. Napier & Sons' patent screw steering gear, fitted to the French Mail Atlantic steam ship "CITY OF PARIS," screw, and now usually fitted by them to large ocean steam ships.
Presented by R. Napier & Sons, Glasgow. 1867.

2. MODEL of a double rudder fitted to stern of a screw steamer. Proposed by Lieut. the Hon. J. Fitzmaurice, R.N.
Lent by Lieut. the Hon. J. Fitmaurice, R.N. 1865.

3. MODEL of a balance rudder.
Proposed and presented by Mr. J. S. Tucker. 1865.

4. MODEL of the stern of a ship fitted with J. Scott Tucker's proposed balance rudder, which can only be unshipped when at right angles with the keel.
Presented by Mr. J. S. Tucker. 1865.

5. MODEL of a flat-bottomed schooner, with an outside tiller. About 1820.
Presented by Mr. J. S. Tucker. 1865.

6. WORKING MODEL of a ship's steering wheel known as the "Niagra" wheel, because fitted on board the United States corvette, "NIAGARA." Designed 1857.
Lent by Mr. Andrew Murray, Chief Engineer, Portsmouth Dockyard. 1867.
Note.—The rudder head is suspended on friction rollers, and the screw gear to move the rudder is of special mechanical arrangement.

7. MODEL balance rudder and arrangement of stern for twinscrew steamships (iron built). Proposed by Mr. C. W. Merrifield, F.R.S.
Lent by Mr. C W. Merrifield, F.R.S. 1869.

8. THREE MODELS showing various systems of "Lumley's" patent rudder.
Invented by H. Lumley, Assoc. I.N.A.
Lent. 1865.

9. MODEL, illustrating Admiral E. A. Inglefield, C.B. invention. The "Hydrostatic" steering apparatus, for heavy ships. The model shows the method adopted in fitting the apparatus to Her Majesty's ship "ACHILLES, 6,000 tons, 1,250 horse-power.
Lent by Admiral E. A. Inglefield, R.N., C.B., F.R.S.
1871.

Note.—Her Majesty's ship "ACHILLES," iron, 20 guns, 1,250 horse-power, armour plated screw, ship. Length 380 ft., breadth 58 ft. 3½ in., depth 21 ft. 1½ in., tonnage 6,121. Laid down at Chatham Yard in August 1861 in a dock, undocked in December 1863. Designed by the Controller's Department, Admiralty, on lines very similiar to Her Majesty's ships "WARRIOR" and "BLACK PRINCE," built in 1860.

The armament is as follows:—

	No.	Prs.
Main deck	{ 8 -	- 100-pr. 6½-ton guns.
	{ 8 -	- 6½-ton rifled guns.
Upper „ -	- 4 -	- 6½-ton „
	20	

Her complement of men is 705.

10. MODEL of a proposed steering apparatus, 1861.
1864.

11. MODEL of "Blake's" plan for adding power to the rudders of gunboats, and vessels of light draught. Designed by Mr. R. Blake, Master Shipwright in H.M.'s Dockyards. 1806–1855.
Presented by the Rev. J. Hardie, Falmouth. 1866.

12. MODEL of "Blake's" plan for constructing a temporary rudder. Designed by Mr. R. Blake, Master Shipwright in H.M's Dockyards, 1806–1855.
Presented by the Rev. J. Hardie, Falmouth. 1866.

13. MODEL of the rudder of a ship of war, wood construction, showing arrangement and scarfing of the timbers, disposition of the braces, rudder head, and other portions.
Designed by Mr. R. Blake, Master Shipwright, H.M.'s Dockyards, 1806–1855.
Presented by Rev. J. Hardie, Falmouth. 1866.

CLASS IX.

Boats :—Ships' Boats, Life Boats and Rafts. All kinds of Boats and Barges used for pleasure.

1. WHOLE MODEL of the Australian life-boat "LADY DALY" built at Adelaide, from design by Mr. W. Taylor, Government Shipwright at that port, about 1867. Length 43 ft. 1 in.; breadth 9 ft.; depth midships 4 ft. 1 in. Scale ¾-inch to 1 foot. The model was presented to His Royal Highness the Duke of Edinburgh, by the Marine Board of South Australia in 1868.

Lent by His Royal Highness the Duke of Edinburgh.
1869.

See also Drawing, No. 67, Class XIV., p. 87.

2. MODEL of the boat built by exhibitors (in 1861) for use of Her Majesty the Queen, and His Royal Highness the Prince Consort, during their visit to Ireland and Lake of Killarney in 1861. The boat was built for Lord Castlerosse. Scale ⅜-inch to 1 foot.

Lent by Searle and Sons, Lambeth. 1872.

3. FOUR MODELS of ships' boats built of steel, with screw propellers, and fitted with engines designed especially by John Penn, Esq., F.R.S., of Greenwich. The boats are planned out for the ships of war, designed by the late Vice-Admiral E. P. Halsted, R.N., in 1866. Each carries two guns forward, protected by moveable iron breastplates.

Presented by R. Napier & Sons, Glasgow. 1867.

1. Launch.

Length - - - 50 feet.
Guns - - - - 2 ten-pounders.
Oars - - - - 22

2. Pinnace.

Length - - - 45 feet.
Guns - - - - 2 ten-pounders.
Oars - - - - 20

3. First Cutter.

Length - - - 35 feet.
Guns - - - - 2 two-pounders.
Oars - - - - 14

4. *Second Cutter.*

Length	-	-	- 30 feet.
Guns -	-	-	- 2 two-pounders.
Oars -	-	-	- 12

See also Class I., No. 4A, p. 11.

4. SECTION, full size, showing portion of strake and gunwale of steel boats, with metal crutch.
Designed by the late Vice-Admiral E. P. Halsted, R.N., in 1866.
Presented by R. Napier & Sons, Glasgow.   1867.

5. STATE BARGE, built at Deptford; length 45 ft., beam 6 ft. 7 in. Has a covered state cabin abaft, and pulls with twelve oars. Built 1702–1707, George Prince of Denmark, Lord High Admiral of England.
Lent by the Admiralty.   1869.

6. STATE BARGE, built 1805, used for conveying the body of Lord Nelson, from Greenwich Hospital to Somerset House, in January 1806. Length 37 feet, breadth 6 ft. 2 in. Pulls with nine oars.
Lent by the Admiralty.   1869.

7. STATE SHALLOP, built 1708. Time of Queen Anne, length 46 feet, beam 6 ft. 7 in. Pulls with ten oars.
Lent by the Admiralty.   1869.

Note.—These three State barges, lent by the Admiralty, are fitted with oars, boat hooks, masts, and gangway boards, complete. They also have awnings, curtains, and cushions, as part of their equipment.

8. MODEL of H.M.'s steam troopship "ORONTES," on a ¼-scale; showing the arrangement of three canting bridges for life boats, with life-boats built on Lamb and White's principle. Also ten of Captain J. W. Hurst's patent life rafts, lashed to ship's sides.
Lent by Messrs. White & Co., Cowes.   1873.

9. SERIES of MODELS (nine in number) of life-boats, built on Lamb and White's principle. Originally designed in 1846 for the Peninsular and Oriental Steam Navigation Company, and since used on board Her Majesty's steam yachts, "VICTORIA and ALBERT," built 1855. "OSBORNE," built 1843. "FAIRY," built 1854. "ALBERTA," built 1863. "ELGIN," built 1849.

CLASS IX.—BOATS.   59

These life-boats are also adopted for Her Majesty's Navy, and the Coast Guard and Trinity House services.
Lent by Messrs. J. White & Co., Cowes, Isle of Wight. 1873.

1. Model, on about ¾-inch scale of a life-boat state barge. Presented by the Peninsular and Oriental Steam Navigation Company in 1857 to the Bey of Tunis.

2. Model, on about ¼-inch scale, of the "MARY WHITE" life-boat. Presented to the boatmen of Broadstars by Mr. Thomas White of Cowes. Used in rescuing the crew of the ship "NORTHERN BELL" off Kingsgate in January 1857.

3. Model of a life-boat on about ¾-inch scale, as furnished to Her Majesty's ships and services. 1846.

4. Model of 36 ft. life-boat, originally designed in 1846, for the Peninsular and Oriental Steam Navigation Company, and now used on board Her Majesty's ships and transports.

5. Model of a life-boat barge, pulling fourteen oars, used in Her Majesty's services. 1859-60.

6. Model of the coast-guard life-boat, ordered to be built, and tried in Dingle Bay, Ireland, in 1864, and now (1873) the pattern boat for coast-guard service round England, Ireland, and Scotland.

7. Model of a yacht's gig fitted as a life-boat. 1872.

8. Model of a yacht's life boat adopted by the Royal Yacht Squadron, New Thames Yacht, and other yachting clubs of the kingdom.

9. Model, on about a ¾-scale, of the construction, arrangement, and fitting of a life-boat built on Messrs. Lamb and White's principle. 1871.
The port side of Model shows disposition of boat's frame and planking.
The starboard side fore bow shows the boat as finished; after end shows the water-tight lining and planking.
The above nine models lent by J. White & Co., Cowes. 1873.

10. NINE MODELS of life-boats, ships' boats and others.
Lent by Messrs. Forrest and Son, Limehouse.   1873.

1. Whale life-boat, for H.M's ship "SYLVIA." Length 28 ft., beam 5 ft. 8 in., depth 2 ft. 6 in., ¾-inch scale.

2. Life-boat cutter for H.M.'s ship "SYLVIA." Length 25 ft., beam 7 ft. 3 in., depth 2 ft. 10 in., ¾-inch scale.

3. Self-righting cutter life-boat, for H.M.'s navy. Length 28 ft., beam 7 ft. 6 in., depth 3 ft. 2 in., ½-inch scale.

4. Life-boat for Trinity Corporation's screw steamer "VESTAL." Length 25 ft., beam 6 ft., depth 2 ft. 4 in., ¾-inch scale.

5. Canoe surf-boat for West Coast of Africa. Length 31 ft., beat 6 ft., depth 2 ft. 4 in., ¾-inch scale.

6. Unsinkable steam launch for ships' and yachts' use. Length 26 ft., beam 6 ft. 6 in., depth 3 ft. 3 in., ¾-inch scale.

7. Special hospital surf-boat for service on West Coast of Africa. New design by Messrs. Forrest and Son, for War Department. Scale 1 inch to 1 foot, length 25 ft., depth 2 ft. 3 in., breadth 5 ft.

8. The yawl "KATE," owner E. E. Middleton, who sailed her alone, all round England in 1869. Scale 1 inch to 1 foot, length 23 ft., breadth 7 ft., depth, 2 ft. 6 in.

9. South Sea whale boat, on a 1 inch to 1 foot scale, length 30 ft. 6 in., breadth 5 ft., depth 2 ft.

Lent by Messrs. Forrest & Sons.   1873.

11. MODEL of the LIFE-BOAT and its transporting Carriage, on about a $\frac{1}{10}$th scale; adopted by the Royal National Life-boat Institution, 14, John Street, Adelphi, London.

Designed for the Institution by Mr. Joseph Prowse in 1861.

Note.—The form of this boat is that usually given to a whale boat with a long flat floor amidships, sides straight, raking stem and stern post, diagonally built of two thicknesses of mahogany and copper fastened. Length, extreme, 33 feet; breadth of beam, 8 feet, and depth inside, 3 feet 4 inches. The boat has five thwarts 2 feet 8 inches apart, and pulls 10 oars double-banked in crutches formed on the thole pin. Extra buoyancy is obtained by the compartments under the deck being filled with water-tight cases packed with cork, detached air cases under the head and stern sheets, and along the sides under the thwarts, and the end air cases in the extremes. It is not probable that this boat could be readily upset, but should such an accident occur provision is made by the sheer of gunwale, raised air cases in the extremes, weight of cork in the bottom, and the iron keel to cause her to right herself. The area of the delivering valves will enable the boat to readily free herself of all water above the deck in 20 seconds, with 47 persons on board.

This life-boat possesses in the highest degree all the qualities which it is desirable that a life-boat should possess, viz., great lateral stability, speed against a heavy sea, facility for launching and taking the shore, immediate self-discharge of any water breaking into it. The advantage of self-righting if upset, strength, and stowage room for a number of passengers.

The carriage consists of a fore and main body. The latter is formed of a keelway, and of side or bilgeways attached to the keelway, and resting on the main axle, the boat's weight being entirely on the rollers of the keelway. Its leading characteristic is that, on the withdrawal of a forelock pin, the fore and main bodies can be detached from each other. The advantages of this arrangement are, that whilst the weight of the boat, when she is launched from the rear end, forms an inclined plane by elevating the keelway, to replace her on the carriage she can be hauled bow foremost up the fore end or longer incline. The bilgeways are needed at the rear end, that the boat may be launched in an upright position with her crew on board, but they are not required at the fore end of the carriage. The boat is hauled off the carriage and launched into the sea by ropes rove through sheeves at the rear end of the carriage, each having one end hooked to a self-detaching hook at the boat's stern, and the other manned by a few persons on the shore, who thus haul the boat and her crew off the carriage and launch them afloat at once, with their oars in their hands; by these means headway may be obtained before the breakers have time to beat the boat broadside on to the beach.

Lent by the Royal National Life-boat Institution.
1865.

12. MODEL. Life-boat. Length 36 ft., breadth 7 ft. 10 in. Designed and lent by Mr. George Turner, late Master Shipwright, Woolwich Dockyard. 1864.

13. MODEL. Life-boat. Length 26 ft. Proposed and lent by Mr. George Turner, late Master Shipwright, Woolwich Dockyard. 1864.

14. MODEL of a Life-boat, designed in 1854. Length 32 ft., breadth 8 ft. 4 in. Scale ¾-in. to 1 foot.
Proposed and presented by Mr. D. Harvey. 1865.

15. MODEL. Illustrating a mode of fitting boats, either singly or in couples, for the disembarkation of troops, horses, and field-guns. This plan was used in the landing of troops in the Crimea, 1854–1856.
    Lent by the inventor, Mr. W. Ladd, Deptford Dockyard. 1864.

16. MODEL of Berthon's patent collapsible troop boats.
    Length - - - 50 feet.
    Beam - - - 14 feet.
    Depth - - - 6 feet 3 inches.
    Oars - - - 12
    Troops - - - 200
    Designed and lent by the Rev. E. L. Berthon, Romsey, Hants. 1867.

17. Two MODELS showing "Fawcus's" new mode of constructing boats, so that several of the same size and shape may be packed together indiscriminately.
    Lent by Mr. G. Fawcus, North Shields. 1866.

18. MODEL of a ship's bulwark fitted with "Fawcus's" patent revolving head davits, for lowering and stowing boats promptly.
    Lent by Mr. George Fawcus, North Shields. 1866.

19. Two BLOCKS. "Fawcus's" improved blocks for lowering ships' boats, with necessary fittings for boat's side, thwarts, &c.
    Presented by Mr. George Fawcus, North Shields. 1865.

20. Two MODELS showing arrangements of boat-chocks with sliding wedge pieces, on Mr. Fawcus's plan.
    Lent by Mr. George Fawcus, North Shields. 1866.

21. MODEL of Captain Hurst's patent bulwark life raft, complete.
    Lent by Captain J. W. Hurst, M.M. 1868.

22. MODEL showing mode of fitting Hurst's patent bulwark life raft to waist-bulwarks of a ship.
    Lent by Captain J. W. Hurst, M.M. 1868.

23. YOKE and CRUTCHES, made from a brass gun taken in Sebastopol, 8th September 1855. Presented to the late Capt. Crispin, R.N.   Lent by Mrs. Crispin. 1865.

CLASS IX.—BOATS.   63

24. WORKING MODEL of Clifford's patent boat-lowering apparatus.
Lent by Mr. A. Battan, Northumberland Alley, E.C.
1874.

Note.—One man performs the operations of unlashing, lowering, and releasing the boat, which cannot cant to one side, nor can one end of the boat enter the water sooner than the other. The boat can be lowered whilst the ship is at full speed, and when she quits the ship steerage way is left, which enables the coxswain to keep her away clear from ship's side.

25. MODEL of the eight-oared "Outrigger" built for the Cambridge University crew in 1860. Length 58 ft., breadth 2 ft. 2 in., depth 1 ft. 1½ in.
Built and lent by Searle & Sons, Lambeth.   1865.

26. MODEL, on 1-in. scale, of the last State Barge built in 1807 for the Lord Mayors of London.
Built and lent by Searle & Sons, Lambeth.   1865.

27. MODEL of an Ice Boat, such as is employed on the Gulf of Finland, the Canadian lakes, &c. The length of the SOKOL (FALCON) is about 25 ft., and at her widest part, where the mast rises, she is 12 ft. broad.
Presented by Mr. John S. Anderson.   1865.

28. WHOLE MODEL of an improved and patented Life-boat, designed by Dr. J. Collis Browne, late Army Medical Staff.
Note.—The boat possesses it is said :—
    a. Extraordinary buoyancy. She affords shelter in the fore and aft projections, to the rescued.
    b. She rides easily in the heaviest sea.
    c. She can be worked to windward by oars alone.
Lent by Dr. J. Collis Browne.   1874.

29. WORKING MODEL of Dr. J. Collis Browne's patented method for lowering ships' boats at sea by means of his patent clip hooks, which release both ends of the boat simultaneously, although one end of the boat take the water first.
Lent by Dr. J. Collis Browne.   1874.

30. CLIP HOOKS, patent. A pair, full size, of Dr. J. Collis Browne's patent clip hooks for letting go ships' boats at sea.
Lent by Dr. J. Collis Browne, 34, Leadenhall Street, E.C.   1874.

31. WORKING MODEL of Hill's patent boat lowering apparatus, and slip hooks, full size. [Messrs. Hill & Clark.]
Lent by Mr. E. J. Hill, 6, Westminster Chambers, Victoria Street, S.W., 1874.

CLASS X.

Instruments for Navigation :—Compasses, Logs, Chronometers, Sextants, &c., Barometers. Nautachometers, Clinometers, &c. Signal Flags, and Ships' Lights.

1. Berthon's patent NAUTACHOMETER or perpetual log, for indicating speed of ships.
    Lent by the Rev. E. L. Berthon, Romsey, Hants. 1867.

2. Berthon's patent bi-fluid CLINOMETER, for showing the oscillation, pitching, and scending of ships, and also their trim.
    Lent by the Rev. E. L. Berthon, Romsey, Hants. 1867.

3. TWO MODELS of ship's binnacles. Proposed for the Navy, 19th March 1853, as an improvement on the square box then in use. Scale 3 in. to 1 foot.
    Presented by Mr. D. Harvey.   1865.

4. SHIP'S COMPASS and BINNACLE. Gray's patent.
    Lent by Mr. John Gray, 26, Strand Street, Liverpool.
                                              1874.

5. SHIP'S COMPASS. Self-registering compass. Mr. J. M. Napier's patent.
    Lent by D. Napier & Sons, Lambeth.   1874.

6. SHIPS' LOGS. Two patent rotating brass logs, with self-acting mile indices and registers, arranged on Massey's principle.
    Manufactured and lent by Mr. L. P. Casella, Holborn.
                                              1874.

7. SET OF STEAM SHIP'S LIGHTS. Three.
    1 port light.
    1 starboard light.
    1 anchor or masthead light. Copper lanterns.
    Lent by Messrs. Stevens & Sons, Southwark Bridge Road.   1874.

CLASS X.—NAVIGATION. 65

8. Two SHIP'S SIGNAL LANTERNS, copper; arranged so as to form with one lantern, a starboard, port, or white riding light. The lanterns are of two sizes, the larger fixes on a stand and revolves, and can be used probably for "flashing," and signalling.
    Lent by Mr. J. S. Starnes, Broad Street, Ratcliff.
                                                    1873.

9. SIGNAL LANTERN, or riding light. Captain Colomb's R.N. riding light, fitted with improved light apparatus and lantern glass or lense, for increasing the brilliancy of the light.
    Lent by Capt. Colomb, R.N.   1873.

10. CHRONOMETERS, 8 and 2 day marine chronometers. Fitted complete.
    Lent by Mr. Victor Kullberg, 105, Liverpool Road, Islington, N.   1874.

11. A set of ships' signal lights and cabin lamps on the "Silber" light system. These lights and lamps comprise ships' starboard, port, and riding lights, signal lights and lamps for saloon and cabin use.
    Lent and manufactured by the Silber Light Co., 49, Whitecross Street, E.C.   1874.

12. FOG-HORN. To be blown by bellows.
    Lent by Mr. J. S. Starnes, Broad Street, Ratcliff. 1873.

13. Specimen of ROPE for hand and deep-sea lead.
                                                    1864.

CLASS XI.

Guns:—Breech and Muzzle-loading Guns. Shot and Shell. Batteries, Turrets, &c.

1. MODEL of 7-in. breech-loading, naval pattern, "Armstrong" rifled gun complete, with sights and vent piece. Manufactured at the Gun Factory, Royal Arsenal, Woolwich, 1867. Purchased 1867.

2. SERIES of ILLUSTRATIONS of GUNS and PROJECTILES adopted in the Royal Navy, 1866–67. Known 1874, as "Armstrong" and "Woolwich" systems for rifled ordnance. From the Royal Arsenal, Woolwich. Purchased 1867.

   1. Model of a 7-inch breech-loading Armstrong gun, with sights and vent piece complete. Manufactured at the Gun Factory, Royal Arsenal, Woolwich.
   2. Wood model of a 7-inch muzzle-loading, wrought-iron, Woolwich rifled naval gun.

SHOT AND SHELL.

3. 13-inch mortar shell, whole.
4. 13-inch mortar shell in section, filled and fused.
5. 10-inch carcass, whole.
6. 150-pr. smooth-bore naval shell.
7. 68-pr., grape shot, Caffin's pattern.
8. 68-pr., solid shot.
9. 7-inch shot for Armstrong's breech-loading gun.
10. 7-inch common shell for Armstrong's breech-loading gun.
11. 7-inch common shell in section, empty.
12. 7-inch segment shell for Armstrong's breech-loading gun.
13. 7-inch segment shell in section, filled, with adapter and Boxer's 9 seconds wood time fuze for rifled ordnance.
14. 7-inch segment shell in section, empty, unleaded.
15. 64-pr. hollow-headed shot, for breech-loading Armstrong gun.
16. 8-inch diaphragm shrapnel shell, for smooth-bore guns.
17. 8-inch diaphragm shrapnel shell, in section, filled, and Boxer's diaphragm wood time fuze.
18. 8-inch diaphragm shrapnel shell in section, empty
19. 8-inch naval shell, whole.
20. 8-inch naval shell in section, empty.
21. 8-inch Martin's shell, whole.

CLASS XI.—GUNS. 67

22. 8-inch Martin's shell in section, showing the filling with molten iron.
23. 12-pr. solid shot.
24. 12-pr. howitzer case shot.
25. 12-pr. segment shell for Armstrong's breech-loading gun.
26. 12-pr. segment shell for Armstrong's breech-loading gun, in section, filled, Dyer's field service percussion, and Armstrong time fuze.
27. Hand grenade for sea service.
28. 12-pr. Congreve rocket and stick complete.
29. 12-pr. Congreve rocket in section.
30. Lubricator for 7-inch breech-loading Armstrong gun, complete, and in section.
31. 8-inch junk wad, used for firing hot shot.
32. 8-inch grummet wad.

METAL FUZES.

33. Boxer's time fuze, 20 seconds, for naval service, whole, in section filled, and empty.
34. Boxer's time fuze, 7½ seconds, for naval service, whole, in section filled, and empty.
35. Armstrong time fuze, for breech-loading guns, whole, in section filled, and empty.
36. Armstrong pillar percussion fuze, for breech-loading guns, whole, in section filled, and empty.
37. Petman's percussion fuze, for naval service, whole, in section filled, and empty.
38. Petman's percussion fuze, for land service, whole, in section filled, and empty.
39. Dyer's field service percussion fuze, whole, in section filled, and empty.

WOOD FUZES.

40. Mortar fuze, large, whole, and in section filled.
41. Mortar fuze, small, whole, and in section filled.
42. Boxer's wood time fuze, 9 seconds, for breech-loading Armstrong guns, whole, and in section filled.
43. Boxer's wood time fuze, 2-inch common, whole, and in section filled.
44. Boxer's wood time fuze, diaphragm shrapnel, whole, and in section filled.
45. Wood fuze for hand grenades.

3. SERIES of MODELS and PROJECTILES, contributed by the Whitworth Armoury Company (Limited), Manchester, showing Sir Joseph Whitworth, Bart., system for rifled guns and projectiles, ranging in calibres from a 2-pr. to a 9-in. or 320-pr. rifled gun.

Proposed for Vice-Admiral Halsted's system of turret and broadside ships of war.   1867.
See Models of Ships, No. 4, Class I., p. 11.

PROJECTILES designed by Sir Joseph Whitworth, Bart., 1867.

1. Longitudinal section of a 3-pr. Whitworth bore, with elongated shell, and rifled sphere, to illustrate the rotation of projectile.
2. 9-inch Whitworth shell, length 45 inches, weight , for firing at close action.
3. 9-inch Whitworth steel shell, length 26 inches, weight, empty, 310 lbs., bursting charge 10 lbs., total 320 lbs.
4. 9-inch rifled sphere.
5. 7-inch Whitworth steel shell, weight 150 lbs., bursting charge 6 lbs.
6. 7-inch shrapnel shell, in section.
7. 7-inch case shot, in section.
8. 7-inch rifled sphere, weight 43·75 lbs.
9. 70-pr. Whitworth shot.
10. 70-pr. rifled sphere, weight 21 lbs.
11. 70-pr. shrapnel shell.
12. 70-pr. shrapnel shell, in section.
13. 70-pr. case shot.
14. 70-pr. case shot, in section.
15. 32-pr. Whitworth shot.
16. 32-pr. rifled sphere, weight 9 lbs.
17. 32-pr. shrapnel shell.
18. 32-pr. shrapnel shell, in section.
19. 32-pr. case shot.
20. 32-pr. case shot, in section.
21. 10-pr. Whitworth shot.
22. 10-pr. rifled sphere.
23. 10-pr. common shell.
24. 10-pr. shrapnel shell.
25. 10-pr. shrapnel shell, in section.
26. 10-pr. case shot.
27. 10-pr. case-shot, in section.
28. 2-pr. common shell.
29. 2-pr. case shot.
30. 2-pr. case shot, in section.
31. 2-pr. rifled sphere.
32. 1-pr. Whitworth steel shot.
33. 1-pr. Whitworth steel shot, with ogival head.
34. 1-pr. Whitworth steel shell.
35. Whitworth tubular cartridge for 9-inch gun, charge 45 lbs.
36. Cross section of Whitworth 7-inch bore, and 7-inch shot, fitted on stand, for the purpose of showing the windage.
37. Small iron plate $\frac{1}{2}$-inch in thickness, showing two penetrations of steel shot, fired at an angle with the Whitworth rifle.

CLASS XI.—GUNS. 69

4. WHOLE MODEL of a twin screw gun-boat, fitted to show method of working the gun turret by chain and winch gear, the patented system of the exhibitor.
Lent by Mr. H. P. D. Cunningham, Gosport. 1872.

5. MODEL of the broadside battery of a ship of war, showing four guns arranged to work by steam power from the deck below the gun deck. The driving drum being kept going, when the different gun ropes are pulled upon, motion is at once given to the guns; on slackening the ropes the motion ceases.
Proposed by Mr. H. P. D. Cunningham, Gosport.
Lent. 1872.

6. MODEL of a broadside battery of a ship of war, showing one gun, designed to be worked from the deck below the gun deck, by means of a revolving shaft, pullies, and sheaves. An endless chain running over these, runs the gun in and out. Revolving bollards in rear part of gun slide, kept in motion by above gear, enables the gun to be traversed in either direction by pulling on the gun ropes when cast round the bollards.
Proposed by Mr. H. P. D. Cunningham, Gosport.
Lent. 1872.

7. MODEL of the broadside battery of a ship of war, showing two guns. The right-hand gun illustrates the traversing gear for the first 12-ton naval gun used on board H.M.S. "EXCELLENT" in 1866, for traversing heavy guns by one man. H.M.S. "MINOTAUR" was fitted on a modified system of the above, for four years.

The same gun in the model also illustrates the method of running in and out of 12-ton guns, used for four years on board H.M.S. "EXCELLENT" and "MINOTAUR."

The left-hand gun shows a proposed plan (1862) for loading the gun in-board; also a slide block compressor, applied to the first 110-pr. Armstrong gun on board H.M.S. "EXCELLENT," 1865. In use two years.

The pivot-bar is shown in the model placed under instead of upon the gun port sill. This method is adopted in the Royal Navy.
Proposed by Mr. H. P. D. Cunningham, Gosport.
Lent. 1872.

8. MODEL in wood of a wrought-iron gun carriage platform. Fitted with Cunningham's patent Bollards, for controlling and working the gun.
Lent by Mr. H. P. D. Cunningham. 1872.

9. MODEL of a forecastle of a ship of war, fitted; showing pivots, racers, &c., to enable the guns and carriages to be shifted from one position to another for firing in any direction.
Purchased from Royal Arsenal, Woolwich. 1867.

1. Model, gun carriage, naval pattern, sliding, for 7-inch breech-loading gun.
2. Model, gun carriage, naval pattern, sliding, for 7-inch muzzle-loading gun.
3. Model, gun carriage, naval pattern, for 32-pr. gun, muzzle-loading, old pattern.
4. Model of a gun carriage, common naval pattern.
5. Model, slide, for 32-pr. gun.
6. Model, slide, for 7-inch breech-loading gun.
7. Model, slide, for 7-inch muzzle-loading gun.

Set of Models of small stores for above:—
   (*a.*) Dismounting chocks.
   (*b.*) Transporting axles with trucks.
   (*c.*) Roller handspikes.
   (*d.*) Wad hook.
   (*e.*) Rammers.
   (*f.*) Sponges.
   (*g.*) Levers (traversing).
   (*h.*) Levers, lifting joints, &c.
   (*i.*) Ramps for raising carriages on to slides.

10. MODEL of a mortar bed, complete, showing the method adopted (1866) for fitting it to the deck of a ship of war so as to obtain an all-round fire. Together with a model in wood of a 13-inch sea service mortar, mounted.
Purchased from Royal Arsenal, Woolwich. 1867.

11. MODEL, showing section of a boat with two guns, and apparatus for working them, on Mr. Walker's plan.
Lent by Mr. J. Walker. 1867.

12. MODEL of a 3-gun battery, showing the working of the guns on Mr. Walker's plan.
Lent by Mr. J. Walker. 1867.

13. MODEL of a floating battery of 3 guns, on Mr. J. Walker's plan.   Lent by Mr. J. Walker. 1867.

14. MODEL of a gun-boat.
Presented by Mr. J. S. Tucker. 1865.

CLASS XI.—GUNS.

15. MODEL, showing portion containing three guns, of main deck battery of the late Vice-Admiral E. P. Halsted's combined turret and broadside ships of war. Designed, 1866.
Presented by Messrs. R. Napier & Sons, Glasgow. 1867.
Note.—The guns are mounted upon iron carriages, designed by Captain T. B. Heathorn, R.A., on his system for muzzle pivoting.
See Class I., No. 4A, page 11, and Class XI., No. 3, page 67.

16. MODEL, a complete working model of R. Napier's patent turret designed to contain two "Whitworth" rifled 9-inch guns, and adopted for the combined turret and broadside armour-plated ships of war, proposed by the late Vice-Admiral E. P. Halsted, R.N., in 1866.
Note.—This model shows the steam turret revolving gear between decks, the method of supporting the turret, the upper and lower decks of ship, and internally the mounting and emplacement of the guns in the turret.
Presented by Messrs. R. Napier & Sons, Glasgow. 1867.
See Models, Class I., No. 4A, page 11.

17. MODEL, in brass, of an old pattern naval service muzzle-loading smooth-bore gun.
Presented by Rev. J. Hardie, Falmouth. 1866.

18. MODEL. Gun fitted, on the inside principle, to H.M.S. "RAPID." Naval service. 1864.

19. MODEL. Two guns on the common principle. Naval service. 1836. 1864.

20. MODEL. Mode of fitting a 32-pounder gun of 25 cwt. in H.M.S. "IMOGEN." Portsmouth Yard, 1831. 1864.

21. MODEL. One gun on carriage. and two on slides, on the inside principle. Naval service.
Proposed by Mr. J. Edye. 1837. 1864.

22. MODEL. Gun and carriage. Naval service. 1864.

23. MODEL. Gun and carriage. Naval service. 1864.

24. MODEL. Gun and carriage, with one pair of trucks, as fitted to H.M.S. "DAPHNE," 18 guns. Built 1838. Naval service. 1864.

25. MODEL. Gun with carriage, fitted with lever to raise and lower the bed and quoin. Naval service. 1864.

26. MODEL. Carronade, on the inside principle, as fitted to H.M.S. "LIBERTY," 16 guns. Built . Naval service. 1864.

27. MODEL 32-pounder carronade, fitted on the inside principle, with slide shortened for quarter deck. Naval service. 1864.

28. PORT, with fittings for a carronade on the non-recoil principle. Naval service. 1864.

29. SHACKLE AND THIMBLE for gun. Proposed for Naval service. 1864.

30. Wood pattern SHACKLE for gun-breeching. Proposed for Naval service. 1864.

31. Projectiles; made of "Atlas" toughened cast steel, in 1864. Broken and slotted to show the density and tough nature of the steel.
The Atlas Steel and Iron Works Co., Sheffield. 1864.
    1. Projectile; spherical shot, 8 inches in diameter.
    2. Projectile; long shot, $12 \times 7\frac{1}{2}$ inches.
    3. Projectile; long shot, $16\frac{3}{4} \times 10\frac{1}{2}$ inches.
    4. Projectile; long shot, $13 \times 8\frac{1}{4}$ inches, broken and slotted transversely.
The above four projectiles, made by the Atlas Steel and Iron Works Co., Sheffield. 1864.

CLASS XII.

Models of Home Vessels.—Fishing and Pilot Boats—Sailing and Steam Barges—Hoys and Lighters—Canal Boats—River Steam Boats—Pleasure Yachts.

---

1. HALF BLOCK MODEL of a WHITBY five-man Fishing Boat. Length, 57 ft.; breadth, 17 ft.; depth, 8 ft. 4 in.; registered tonnage, 45 tons.
 Lent by Mr. T. Turnbull, A.I.N.A.   1869.

2. HALF BLOCK MODEL of a "COBLE" of the Yorkshire coast. Each five-man fishing boat carries two cobles. The flat after end allows them to be easily beached. When under sail a rudder projecting 4 ft. below the stern is used.
 Lent by Mr. T. Turnbull, A.I.N.A.   1869.

3. HALF BLOCK MODEL of a fishing MULE of the Yorkshire coast. Coble form forward; yawl form aft.
 Length, 33 ft. 9 in.; breadth, 10 ft.; depth, 4 ft. 9 in. Scale, 1 in. to 1 ft.
 Lent by Mr. T. Turnbull, A.I.N.A., Whitby.   1871.

4. WHOLE MODEL, rigged, of a Thames sailing BARGE. Built 1855. Length 70 ft.; breadth 16 ft.; depth 6 ft.
 Built and lent by Searle & Sons, Lambeth.   1865.

5. WHOLE MODEL of Dr. J. Collis Browne's sailing fore and aft schooner yacht "KALAFISH." Tons 60. Royal Cinque Ports Yacht Club.
 See Model, No. 37, Class I., p. 20.
 Lent by Dr. J. Collis Browne, 34, Leadenhall Street.
                 1874.

CLASS XIII.

Foreign Craft and Vessels of all kinds.

1. WHOLE MODEL, rigged, of the Viceroy of Egypt's yacht, for the river Nile.
    Presented by the Egyptian Commissioner for the Paris Exhibition of 1867.   1868.

2. WHOLE MODEL of the American river side-wheel steamer "EMPIRE," of the New York and Albany line of steamers.   Presented by Mr. D. Lapraike.   1868.
    Note.—This model shows particularly the ship's construction, the disposition of the passenger accommodation, and the emplacement of the boilers, steering wheel house, &c.

3. MODEL, rigged, of a Ceylon boat. Length 14 in., breadth 1 inch. Outrigger, $7\frac{1}{4}$ inches over all.
    Presented by Mr. T. D. E. Gibson.   1865.

4. MODEL, rigged, of a Cingalese outrigger canoe. Length 2 ft. 2 inch, breadth $1\frac{1}{4}$ inch. Over all, 10 inches, outrigger.
    Lent by Mr. Thos. F. Dodd.   1868.

5. WHOLE MODELS. Three masted Chinese junk. Six Chinese boats.
    Length of the junk, 21 in., breadth $5\frac{1}{4}$ in.
    Length of the boats, 20 in., breadth 4 in.

,,	,,	$17\frac{1}{2}$,,	,,	$3\frac{1}{2}$,,
,,	,,	14 ,,	,,	4 ,,
,,	,,	10 ,,	,,	$2\frac{1}{4}$,,
,,	,,	9 ,,	,,	3 ,,
,,	,,	$4\frac{1}{2}$,,	,,	$1\frac{1}{2}$,,

    Presented by Mr. J. Pybus.   1868.

6. WHOLE MODEL of a three-masted Chinese junk, rigged. Length 4 ft. 2 in., breadth 11 in., depth 7 in. The model shows upper deck fittings, hatchways, cooking galley, cabins, &c.
    Presented by Mr. W. T. Lay.   1870.

7. MODEL of an ancient Maltese galley, supposed to have belonged to one of the Grand Masters of the Knights of Malta, together with a small painting containing a representation of the galley, and probably of contemporary date

CLASS XIII.—FOREIGN CRAFT. 75

with it. Length of model, 6 ft. 2 in., breadth 14½ in., depth 6 in.
    Lent by Mr. W. Ladd, late Master Shipwright, Deptford Dockyard.   1864.

8. WHOLE MODEL of a Bombay pleasure Boat or yacht, full rigged, two-masted boat, with latteen sails, running gear, deck fittings, &c. Length of model 3 ft. 7 in., beam 7¼ in., extreme depth 7 in. Scale about 1 in. to 1 ft.
    Presented by H.R.H. the Duke of Edinburgh.   1871.

9. MODEL of a Fiji or Feejee double Sailing Canoe, rigged with mast and sails, complete. Made by natives of the Fiji or Feejee islands. Length of major canoe 3 ft. 3 in.; minor canoe 2 feet 11 in. Extreme breadth 18½ in.
    Presented by Sir D. Cooper, F.R.G.S.   1872.

10. MODEL of the Nile dakabeah "MARIANNE." Constructed by Rev. A. J. Foster. Scale ¼ in. to 1 ft.
    Lent by Rev. A. J. Foster.   1873.

11. TREE CANOE. From the Hudson's Bay Territory. Length 19 feet, breadth 2 ft. 8¼ in.
    Presented by the Hudson's Bay Company.   1870.

12. ESQUIMAUX CANOE. From the Hudson's Bay Territory. Length 20 ft., breadth 1 ft. 6 in.
    Presented by the Hudson's Bay Company.   1870.

13. BIRCH BARK CANOE. From the Hudson's Bay Territory. Length 19 ft., breadth 2 ft. 10½ in.
    Presented by the Hudson's Bay Company.   1870.
    Note. — Nine paddles belonging to above three canoes, from Hudson's Bay Territory.
    Presented by the Hudson's Bay Company.   1870.

14. MODEL, rigged, of a Cingalese outrigger Canoe. Length extreme, 3 feet 4¼ inches; beam, ¼ inch; length of outrigger, 2 feet 2 inches extreme; extreme breadth over all, 15 inches.
    Presented by Mr. W. R. Page, Putney.   1874.

CLASS XIV.

Paintings, Drawings, Photographs, of Ships, and of Subjects in connexion with them.

Oil Paintings.

1. Stern View of H.M.S. "Royal George," 1st rate, 100 guns, length 178 ft. 0 in., breadth 51 ft. 9½ in., depth 21 ft. 6 in., tonnage 2,041. Laid down at Woolwich Yard in 1746, launched in 1756, overset 29th August 1782, "she being heeled to come at the pipe that leads to the well."
The complement of men was 850.
Drawn by Josh. Williams, painted by Josh. Marshall, 1774.
Presented by Her Majesty.   1864.

2. Bow View of H.M.S. "Royal George" (same ship as the preceding).
Drawn by J. Binmer, painted by Josh. Marshall, 1774.
Presented by Her Majesty.   1864.

3. Stern View of H.M.S. "Victory," 1st rate, 100 guns, length 174 ft. 9 in., breadth 50 ft. 6 in., depth 20 ft. 6 in., tonnage 1,921. Built at Portsmouth Yard in 1737. Lost in the English Channel in the night between the 4th and 5th October 1744, when Admiral Balchin and the crew of upwards of 1,000 men perished.
Drawn by Josh. Williams, painted by Josh. Marshall, 1744.
Presented by Her Majesty.   1864.

4. Bow View of H.M.S. "Victory," (same ship as the preceding).
Drawn by J. Binmer, painted by Josh. Marshall, 1774.
Presented by Her Majesty.   1864.

5. Stern View of H.M.S. "Barfleur," 2nd rate, 90 guns, length 177 ft. 8 in., breadth 50 ft. 5 in., depth 21 ft., tonnage 750. Laid down at Chatham Yard in 1762, launched in 1768, broken up in 1819.
The complement of men was 750.
Drawn by Josh. Williams, painted by Josh. Marshall, 1774.
Presented by Her Majesty.   1864.

CLASS XIV.—PAINTINGS AND DRAWINGS.   77

6. Bow View of H.M.S. "Barfleur" (same ship as the preceding).
    Drawn by J. Binmer, painted by Josh. Marshall, 1774.
    Presented by Her Majesty.   1864.

7. Stern View of H.M.S. "Royal Oak," 3rd rate, 74 guns, length 168 ft. 6 in., breadth 46 ft. 9 in., depth 20 ft., tonnage 1,606. Laid down at Devonport Yard in 1766, launched in 1769, broken up in 1815.
    The complement of men was 650.
    Drawn by Josh. Williams, painted by Josh. Marshall, 1774.
    Presented by Her Majesty.   1864.

8. Bow View of H.M.S. "Royal Oak" (same ship as the preceding).
    Drawn by J. Binmer, painted by Josh. Marshall, 1774.
    Presented by Her Majesty.   1864.

9. Stern View of H.M.S. "Intrepid," 3rd rate, 64 guns, length 159 feet. 6 in., breadth 44 ft. 5 in., depth 19 ft., tonnage 1,374. Laid down at Woolwich Yard in 1767, launched in 1770, sold in 1828.
    The complement of men was 500.
    Drawn by Josh. Williams, painted by Josh. Marshall, 1774.
    Presented by Her Majesty.   1864.

10. Bow View of H.M.S. "Intrepid" (same ship as the preceding).
    Drawn by J. Binmer, painted by Josh Marshall, 1774.
    Presented by Her Majesty.   1864.

11. Stern View of H.M.S. "Portland," 4th rate, 50 guns, length 146 ft., breadth 40 ft. 6 in., depth 17 ft. 6 in., tonnage 1,044. Laid down at Sheerness Yard in 1767, launched in 1770, sold in 1807.
    The complement of men was 350.
    Drawn by Josh. Williams, painted by Josh. Marshall, 1774.
    Presented by Her Majesty.   1864.

12. Bow View of H.M.S. "Portland" (same ship as the preceding).
    Drawn by J. Binmer, painted by Josh. Marshall, 1774.
    Presented by Her Majesty.   1864.

13. STERN VIEW of H.M.S. "EXPERIMENT," 4th rate, 50 guns, length 140 ft. 9 in., breadth 38 ft. 8¼ in., depth 16 ft. 7 in., tonnage 923. Laid down at Messrs. Adams & Co.'s yard, on the Thames, in 1772, launched in 1774. Dismasted in a gale of wind, and taken the 22nd September 1779 by the French fleet, on her passage from New York to Savannah.

The complement of men was 300.

Drawn by Josh. Williams, painted by Josh. Marshall, 1775.

Presented by Her Majesty. 1864.

14. Bow VIEW of H.M.S. "EXPERIMENT" (same ship as the preceding).

Drawn by J. Binmer, painted by Josh. Marshall, 1775.

Presented by Her Majesty. 1864.

15. STERN VIEW of H.M.S. "AMBUSCADE," 5th rate, 32 guns, length 126 ft. 3 in., breadth 35 ft. 1¾ in., depth 12 ft. 2 in., tonnage 684. Laid down at Messrs. Adams & Co.'s yard, on River Thames in 1771, launched in 1773. Taken by the "BAYONAISE" in December 1798, afterwards retaken and broken up in 1813.

The complement of men was 220.

Drawn by Josh. Williams, painted by Josh. Marshall, 1775.

Presented by Her Majesty. 1864.

16. Bow VIEW of H.M.S. "AMBUSCADE" (same ship as the preceding).

Drawn by J. Binmer, painted by Josh. Marshall.

Presented by Her Majesty. 1864.

17. STERN VIEW of H.M.S. "ENTERPRIZE," 6th rate, 28 guns, length 120 ft. 6 in., breadth 33 ft. 6 in., depth 11 ft., tonnage 594. Laid down at Deptford Yard in 1771, launched in 1774, broken up in 1807.

The complement of men was 200.

Drawn by Josh. Williams, painted by Josh. Marshall, 1775.

Presented by Her Majesty. 1864.

18. Bow VIEW of H.M.S. "ENTERPRIZE" (same ship as the preceding).

Drawn by J. Binmer, painted by Josh. Marshall, 1775.

Presented by Her Majesty. 1864.

CLASS XIV.—PAINTINGS AND DRAWINGS.   79

19. STERN VIEW of H.M.S. "SPHINX," 6th rate, 20 guns, length 108 ft., breadth 30 ft., depth 9 ft. 8 in., tonnage 429. Laid down at Portsmouth Yard in 1773, launched in 1775. Taken by the French in 1779, and retaken in December 1779 by the "PROSERPINE." Broken up at Portsmouth in 1811.
  The complement of men was 160.
  Drawn by Josh. Williams, painted by Josh. Marshall, 1775.
    Presented by Her Majesty.   1864.

20. BOW VIEW of H.M.S. "SPHINX" (same ship as the preceding).
  Drawn by J. Binmer, painted by Josh. Marshall, 1775.
    Presented by Her Majesty.   1864.

21. STERN VIEW of H.M.S. "KINGFISHER,". sloop, 14 guns, length 96 ft. 8½ in., breadth 26 ft. 10 in., depth 12 ft. 10 in., tonnage 302. Laid down at Chatham Yard in 1769, launched in 1770, burnt at Rhode Island, 30th July 1778.
  The complement of men was 125.
  Drawn by Josh. Williams, painted by Josh. Marshall, 1775.
    Presented by Her Majesty.   1864.

22. BOW VIEW of H.M.S. "KINGFISHER" (same ship as preceding).
  Drawn by J. Binmer, painted by Josh. Marshall, 1775.
    Presented by Her Majesty.   1864.

23. Two PAINTINGS of ships on copper. These paintings were used in the Royal Nursery, for the instruction of Prince William Henry, afterwards King William IV.
    Presented by Mr. F. A. B. Bonney.   1865.

24. Two OIL PAINTINGS of the "GREAT BRITAIN," at "Low water" and "High water," by J. Walter, 1847.
    Lent by Capt. Claxton, R.N.   1865.
  Note.—The "GREAT BRITAIN," 3,600 tons, was exposed 11 months in Dundrum Bay, Ireland, and nearly submerged at every high tide; the sea in south-westerly and southerly gales making a clear breach all over her.
    The breakwater here represented, combined with the "GREAT BRITAIN" admirable build, saved the vessel. The design for the breakwater was

Brunel's, and it consisted of 8,000 large faggots, 3 ft. in diameter and 12 or 13 ft. long, placed about the stern and exposed quarter, loaded with stones, and backed by two rows of birch trees, about 60 ft. long. The "GREAT BRITAIN" was got off by Capt. Claxton, R.N., in 1848.

25. BATTLE OF LEPANTO, Oct. 7, 1571. The great naval engagement between the combined fleets of Spain, Venice, Genoa, Malta, and Pius V.; and the whole maritime force of the Turks. By Bonaventura Peters.
Lent by Mr. T. Dyer Edwardes.   1865.

26. BATTLE OF SOLEBAY, May 28, 1672, fought between the fleets of England and France on one side, and the Dutch on the other, the former commanded by the Duke of York, afterwards James II.
Lent by Mr. T. Dyer Edwardes.   1865.

27. BATTLE OF THE DOGGERBANK, in 1781, between the English and Dutch fleets. By T. Luny. 1781.
Lent by Mr. T. Dyer Edwardes.   1865.

28. MEN-OF-WAR IN PORT, by Anderson (b. 1757, d. 1837).
Lent by Mr. T. Dyer Edwardes.   1865.

29. SHIPPING, by Wimont. Painting.
Lent by Mr. T. Dyer Edwardes.   1865.

30. MALTESE GALLEY. Painting.
Lent by Mr. T. Dyer Edwardes.   1865.

31. OIL PAINTING of a Dutch man-of-war. By A. Stork.
Lent by Mr. T. Dyer Edwardes.   1868.

32. OIL PAINTING of an action between Maltese and Algerine vessels. By Vanvitelli, 1647–1736.
Lent by Mr. T. Dyer Edwardes.   1868.

33. OIL PAINTING of Maltese men-of-war at anchor. By Vanvitelli, 1647--1736.
Lent by Mr. T. Dyer Edwardes.   1868.

34. PICTURE of Dutch men-of-war. By Johannes Coesermans.
Lent by Mr. T. Dyer Edwardes.   1868.

CLASS XIV.—PAINTING AND DRAWINGS. 81

35. OIL PAINTING of Dutch shipping. By Van Ass.
Lent by Mr. T. Dyer Edwardes. 1868.

See also series of Engravings, No. 60, page 83.
Presented by Mr. T. Dyer Edwardes. 1868.

36. PAINTING IN OIL. A launch at Deptford Dockyard English, middle of the 18th centy. By J. Cleveley.
Bought. Science and Art Department. 1867.

37. The American packet ship "WARREN" under jury masts and temporary rudder. These were fitted after her own had been carried away by a storm in the Mid-Atlantic, and enabled her to reach England in safety.
Painted by Mr. George Mears. 1868.

38. PENCIL DRAWING of the hull of a man-of-war, "SOVEREIGN OF THE SEAS," by William Van de Velde (b. 1663, at Amsterdam, d. 1707).
Presented by Mr. George Smith. 1865.

39. A DRAWING of the port disposition of the frame of H.M.S. "AMETHYST," wrecked in Bovesand Bay, Plymouth Sound, in 1811. Her top side timbers had been continuously bolted, when last repaired according to the plan proposed by the late "Joseph Tucker," Esq., Surveyor of the Navy, and after having been 21 days on the rocks during a gale of wind, she was floated off to Plymouth Dockyard, with unbroken sheer.
Presented by Mr. John Scott Tucker. 1865.

40. DRAWING of a proposed 4-decked ship, the "DUKE OF KENT," 170 guns, planned and proposed in 1809 by the late "Joseph Tucker," Esq., Surveyor of the Navy, 1813–1831.
Presented by Mr. John Scott Tucker. 1865.
The drawing shows lines, draught, profile, stern elevation, &c. See Model, No. 8, Class I., p. 30.

DRAWINGS, &c. The following (15), lent (1868) by Mr. John Scott Russell, F.R.S., are all of ships built by him.

42. LONGITUDINAL DRAWING of the "GREAT EASTERN," steamship. Built 1857.

F 2

43. DRAWING, cross section of the "GREAT EASTERN" steamship.

44. WATER-COLOUR DRAWING of the "GREAT EASTERN" steamship, off the Isle of Wight.

45. OIL PAINTING of the "GREAT EASTERN" steamship, going through the Downs.

46. OIL PAINTING of the "GREAT EASTERN" steamship, leaving the river Medway, off Sheerness.
Note.—The "GREAT EASTERN" steamship was laid down in 1852, and launched in 1857, at Millwall. See model, No. 44, Class III., p. 40.

47. OIL PAINTING of the Royal West India Mail Company's fleet in Southampton Water.

48. WATER-COLOUR DRAWING of the Sydney and Melbourne Royal Mail Steam Packet Company's paddle steamer "PACIFIC," tons 1,470, horse-power 500.

49. DRAWINGS of the Engines, Boilers, and Wheels of the Sydney and Melbourne Royal Mail Steam Packet Company's paddle-wheel steamer "PACIFIC," 500 horse-power.

50. WATER-COLOUR DRAWING of the Prussian man-of-war paddle steamer, "DANTZIC;" guns 12 ; horse-power 400 ; and Prussian frigates.

51. WATER-COLOUR DRAWING of the Prussian paddle gun-boats "NIX" and "SALAMANDER."

52. WATER-COLOUR DRAWING of "DANTZIC," "NIX," and "SALAMANDER," Prussian war ships, at gunnery practice.

53. WATER-COLOUR DRAWING of a four-masted screw steamer.

54. WATER-COLOUR DRAWING of a four-masted sailing ship in a gale of wind.

55. WATER-COLOUR DRAWING of a screw steamer.

56. WATER-COLOUR DRAWING of the launch of a frigate at Millwall.
   The preceding 15 Drawings lent by Mr. John Scott Russell, F.R.S.   1868.

CLASS XIV.—PAINTINGS AND DRAWINGS.

ENGRAVINGS AND DRAWINGS.

60. Series of ENGRAVINGS (23 in number) illustrating ships-of-war of early periods and of various countries.
Presented by T. Dyer Edwardes, Esq.   1868.
The principal engravings are—
An English second-rate ship-of-war of the smaller class.   1670.
A French second-rate.   1670.
A Spanish second-rate.   1670.
A Dutch second-rate.   1670.
The English fleet.   1342.
A Dutch ship-of-war.
Three English vessels, ships-of-war: The "GREAT HARRY," 1503; the "ROYAL JAMES;" the "ROYAL GEORGE," 1756.
A wicker boat of the ancient Britons.
The English war ship "HENRI GRACE À DIEU," 1520.   1,000 tons burthen.
The other engravings represent ships of ancient Rome, Maltese and Italian galleys, fire ships, &c.
See also Oil Paintings, page 80.
Presented by Mr. T. Dyer Edwardes.   1868.

COLOURED CHART. British flags.
Presented by Mr. James Reynolds.   1864.

61. CHART, partly coloured, illustrating the flags of all nations, the rigging and sails of a ship, and varieties of shipping.   Presented by Mr. James Reynolds.   1864.

62. ENGRAVINGS of "Lumley's" rudder, showing its modifications.
Lent by Mr. H. Lumley, Assoc. I.N.A.   1865.

63. COLOURED ENGRAVINGS of Capt. E. Bedford's, R.N., uniform code for the distinction of buoys by colour.
Presented by Capt. E. G. Bedford, R.N.   1867.

64. TWO ENGRAVINGS showing elevation, longitudinal section, &c. of improved life-boats, arranged to pack one in the other.
Presented by Mr. George Fawcus, North Shields.
1868.

65. DRAWINGS (lithographs). Lent by Mr. John Scott Russell, F.R.S., 1868, illustrating practical shipbuilding. 59 Plates.

Plate 22. Practical Ship Construction, Iron.
   Midship section of an iron ship, showing internal construction and iron bulk-head.

Plate 33. Projections.
   Lines. Paddle-wheel steamer. Port view.

Plate 34. Projections.
   Lines. Paddle-wheel steamer. Starboard view.

Plate 35. Projections.
   Lines. Paddle-wheel steamer. Port view.

Plate 36. Projections.
   Lines. Paddle-wheel steamer. Starboard view.

Plate 37. Projections.
   Lines. Screw steamer.

Plate 38. Projections.
   Lines. Screw steamer. Port view.

Plate 39. Iron Shipbuilding.
   The "GREAT EASTERN" steamship. Built 1857. Lines.

Plate 40. Iron Shipbuilding.
   The "GREAT EASTERN" steamship. Built 1857. Enlarged body plan. Lines.

Plate 51. Iron Shipbuilding.
   The "GREAT EASTERN" steamship. Built 1857. Iron deck plan.

Plate 57. Lines and Structure.
   Screw steam yacht, showing longitudinal sections, lines, deck plan, midship section, and sail draft.

Plate 58, 59. Paddle-wheel steamships.
   Royal steam yacht.
   58, hull complete. Upper deck plan. Sail draft.
   59, longitudinal through section. Lower deck plan.

Plate 60, 61. Paddle-wheel Steamships.
   Extreme shallow-water navigation.
   60, longitudinal through section and deck plan.
   61, hull complete, and deck plan.

Plate 62. Paddle-wheel steamships.
   Channel mail packet. Longitudinal through section. Deck plan.

Plate 64. Screw steamships.
   Cargo trader, with water ballast hold. Longitudinal through section. Deck plan.

Plate 66. Screw steamships.
   Screw collier. Longitudinal through section. Two deck plans.

Plate 67, 68. Paddle-wheel steamships.
   Irish trader.
   67, hull complete. Deck plan.
   68, longitudinal through section. Deck plan.

CLASS XIV. — PAINTINGS AND DRAWINGS. 85

Plate 69, 70. Paddle-wheel steamships.
Mediterranean trader and mail ship.
   69, longitudinal through section.
   70, two deck plans.

Plate 71, 72, 73, 74. Screw steamships.
Baltic trader and mail packet.
   71, longitudinal through section.
   72, upper deck plan.
   73, under deck plan.
   74, hull plan.

Plate 75. Screw steamships.
Auxiliary screw, China clipper. Longitudinal through section. Plan of iron deck.

Plate 83, 84. Ships of war.
Screw gun-boat.
   83, hull, sail draft.
   84, longitudinal section. Deck plan.

Plate 77, 78, 79. Screw steamships.
Australian passenger trader.
   77, longitudinal through section.
   78, upper deck plan.
   79, passengers' cabins and saloon plan.

Plate 86, 87, 88. Ships of war, iron.
Paddle-wheel gunboat.
   86, hull, drawing.
   87, longitudinal through section.
   88, deck plan.

Plate 94. Iron Shipbuilding.
The "GREAT EASTERN" steamship. Built 1857. External profile.

Plate 95. Iron Shipbuilding.
The "GREAT EASTERN" steamship, longitudinal through section.

Plate 96. Iron Shipbuilding.
The "GREAT EASTERN" steamship. First deck plan.

Plate 97. Iron Shipbuilding.
The "GREAT EASTERN" steamship. Second deck plan.

Plate 98. Iron Shipbuilding.
The "GREAT EASTERN" steamship. Third deck plan.

Plate 99. Iron Shipbuilding.
The "GREAT EASTERN" steamship. Fourth deck plan.

Plate 100. Iron Shipbuilding.
The "GREAT EASTERN" steamship. Fifth deck plan.

Plate 101. Iron Shipbuilding.
The "GREAT EASTERN" steamship. Built 1857. Cross section through paddle engine room.

Plate 102. Iron Shipbuilding.
The "GREAT EASTERN" steamship. Cross section through boiler room; cross section through screw engine room.

Plate 103. Iron Shipbuilding.
The "GREAT EASTERN" steamship. Built 1857. Sail drafts, sections.

Plate 104. Iron Shipbuilding.
The "GREAT EASTERN" steamship. Sail draft; half plan, upper deck, disposition of boats, cranes, &c.

Plate 105. Iron Shipbuilding.
The "GREAT EASTERN" steamship. Built 1857. Launching.

Plate 112. Wave-line Principles.
Forms of least resistance.

Plate 113. Wave-line Principles.
Pure wave-lines, body plan, profile, water lines, profile of stern on the vertical system, stern water-line, body stern plan, combined stern body plan.

Plate 114. Wave-line Principles.
1. Reconciled wave-lines, pure wave-line frame, double bow, profile water-lines, body plan.
2. Reconciled stern with pure wave-line form bow, water-lines, body plan.
3. Reconciled bow with reconciled stern, profile, water-lines, body plan.

Plate 115. Wave line Principles.
Compromised wave-lines, bow and stern forms, water-lines, body plans.

Plate 120. Paddle-wheel steamships. Iron.
Pacific royal mail ships.
Lines. Longitudinal through section.

Plate 123, 124. Paddle-wheel steamships. Iron.
Holyhead Royal Irish mail.
123. Longitudinal through section, upper deck plan.
124. Two deck plans, hold plan.

Plate 127. Paddle-wheel steamships. Iron.
French mail Brazilian liners.
Longitudinal through section. Two deck plans.

Plate 133. Ocean passenger and cargo ships.
Screw steamships. Iron.
Longitudinal through section. Two deck plans.

Plate 144. Ships of war. Iron armour ships.
Captain Cowper Coles' cupola ship.
Fig. 1-4. Plans of arrangement for cupolas and deck.
Fig. 5. Elevation, sail draft.
Fig. 6. Midship section, sail draft.

CLASS XIV.—PAINTINGS AND DRAWINGS. 87

Plate 145. Ships of war. Iron armour.
Captain Cowper Coles' cupola ship. (Gun turrets.)
    Figs. 1 and 3. Cross sections of turrets.
    Fig. 6. Elevation of turret.
    Figs. 2 and 4. Interior plans of turret.
    Fig. 7. Exterior plan, turret.
Plate. Lloyd's Register of British and foreign shipping. Illustrations of rules for building iron ships, 1863 ; showing keelsons, side elevation, midship framings, beams, deck plans.
The foregoing 59 plates, illustrating practical shipbuilding.
    Lent by Mr. John Scott Russell, F.R.S.   1868.

67. LITHOGRAPH. Plans and sections of life-boat "LADY DALY," built in Austrialia. Length 43 ft. 1 in., breadth 9 ft., depth midships 4 ft. 1 in. Designed by W. Taylor, Government Shipwright, Port Adelaide, South Australia. About 1867.
    Lent by H.R.H. The Duke of Edinburgh, 1869.
    See Model of boat "LADY DALY," Class IX., No. 1, p. 57.

68. DRAWING of the Pacific Steam Navigation Company's Royal Mail screw steamship "BRITANNIA."
Designed, engined, and built by Messrs. Laird Brothers, Birkenhead, 1873.
    Profile.—Sail draft, longitudinal section.
    Plans of spar, main, and lower decks.
    Engine and boiler rooms.
    Length 399 ft., breadth 43 ft., depth 35 ft. 3 in. Tons, o.m. 3,670. Horse-power 600.
    Has accommodation for 748 passengers.
    See also Model of ship, Class I., No. 19, p. 16.
    Lent by Messrs. Laird Brothers, Shipbuilders, Birkenhead.   1874.

69. Two COLOURED ENGRAVINGS of the screw steamship "ARCHIMEDES" at sea, on 14th May 1839. Built in 1839 by Mr. H. Wimshurst, of Limehouse, for "The Ship Propeller Company."
The ship fitted with Mr. Francis Pettit Smith's screw propeller.
    Dimensions of ship "ARCHIMEDES" were:—
    Extreme length, 125 ft. ; extreme breadth, 22 ft. 6 in. ; depth, 13 ft. ; tons, 240 ; draught of water, 10 feet aft, 9 feet forward.

The engines were of 80 horse-power.
Diameter of screw, 5 ft. 9 in.; length of screw, 5 feet.
Screw was driven by vertical engines and multiplied wheel gearing.
The drawings show also profile of the ship.
Lent by Mr. Henry Wimshurst, Anerley Road. 1873.

70. LITHOGRAPH, illustrating methods of raising sunken ships and wrecks, by means of Messrs. Siebe, Gorman, and Christy's patent ship-raising iron pontoon.
Messrs. Siebe and Gorman, Submarine Engineers, Denmark Street, Soho.
Presented by Messrs. T. Christy & Co., 155, Fenchurch Street, E.C. 1873.

71. LITHOGRAPH. Longitudinal elevation and cross sections illustrating Captain Archibald Thomson's proposals for the improved construction of screw steam ships.
See Model, No. 43, Class III., p. 40.
Lent by Mr. A. Thomson. 1874.

COLOURED DRAWINGS.

72. DRAWINGS of racing and pleasure boats, built by Messrs. Searle & Sons, Stangate, Lambeth. Lent 1873.
Single sculling outrigger gig.
Length, 24 ft. Breadth, 2 ft. 8 in.
Sailing canoe.
Length, 14 ft. Breadth, 2 ft. 8 in.
Four-oared gig with raised chocks.
Length, 24 ft. Breadth, 3 ft. 5 in.
Four-oared outrigger gig.
Length, 38 ft. Breadth, 2 ft. 5 in.
Lake boat, sailing or rowing.
Length, 20 ft. Breadth, 4 ft. 9 in.
Dinghee.
Length, 12 ft. Breadth, 4 ft. 6 in.
Eight-oared racing outrigger.
Length, 57 ft. Breadth, 2 ft. 2 in.
Four-oared racing outrigger.
Length, 42ft. Breadth, 1 ft. 9 in.
Pair-oared racing outrigger.
Length, 35 ft. Breadth, 1 ft. 5 in.
Single sculling skiff.
Length, 22 ft. Breadth, 3 ft. 6 in.
Pair-oared or double sculling gig.
Length, 26 ft. Breadth, 3 ft. 10 in.
Sailing canoe.
Length, 15 ft. Breadth, 3 ft. 2 in.
Pair-oared or double sculling gig.
Length, 24 ft. Breadth, 3 ft. 8 in.

Pair-oared or double sculling gig.
Length, 24 ft. Breadth, 3 ft. 8 in.
Randan skiff.
Length, 27 ft. Breadth, 4 ft. 6 in.
Pair-oared skiff.
Length, 20 ft. Breadth, 4 ft. 6 in.
Racing outrigger, with sliding seat.
Length, 32 ft. Breadth, 1 ft.
Pair-oared or double sculling outrigger gig.
Length, 28 ft. Breadth, 2 ft. 6 in.
Sailing gig, with centre board.
Length, 20 ft. Breadth, 4 ft. 6 in.
Four-oared gig.
Length, 35 ft. Breadth, 3 ft. 5 in.
Four-oared gig.
Length, 35 ft. Breadth, 4 ft. 6 in.
Rob Roy canoe.
Length, 14 ft. Breadth, 2 ft. 2 in.
Single sculling gig.
Length, 18 ft. Breadth, 3 ft. 6 in.

Lent by Messrs' Searle & Sons, Drawings of Boats.
1873.

73. TWO COLOURED DRAWINGS of the first screw steamship "ARCHIMEDES" on her voyage from London to Portsmouth in May 1839.
Presented to the late Vice-Admiral E. P. Halsted R.N., and by him bequeathed to Museum.
These drawings will be found in the case of Ship Models presented by Messrs. R. Napier & Sons, Glasgow, in 1867. See Class III., No. 12, page 30.

PHOTOGRAPHS.

80. PHOTOGRAPH of the fore topsail of Lord Nelson's ship "VICTORY," after the battle of Trafalgar in 1805.
Presented by Mr. S. Willcocks, Master Sailmaker, H.M. Dockyard, Sheerness. 1868.

81. SIX PHOTOGRAPHS, presented, 1869, by Messrs. R. Napier and Sons, Glasgow, of ships built by them, as follows:—
1. H.M.'s iron screw troopship "MALABAR." Built and engined, 1867, by R. Napier & Sons. Length, 360 ft.; breadth, 49 ft.; depth, 22 ft. 4 in.; tonnage, 4,173; horsepower, 700. See Model of H.M.'s ship "JUMNA," Class I., p. .
2. Armour-clad monitor "DE TYGER." Built, 1868, by R. Napier & Sons, for the Royal Dutch Government. Length, 187 ft.; breadth, 44 ft.; depth, 11 ft. 6 in.; tonnage, 1,612; horse-power, 140.

3. Armour-clad monitor "DE BUFFEL." Built 1868, by R. Napier & Sons, for the Royal Dutch Government. Length, 205 ft.; breadth, 40 ft.; depth, 24 ft.; tonnage, 1,472; horse-power, 400; twin screw.

4. Iron-clad screw frigates "OSMAN," "GHAZY," and Others on same lines. Built, 1866, by R. Napier & Sons, for the Imperial Ottoman Government. Tonnage, 4,221; horse-power, 900.

5. Screw steamships "PEREIRE" and "VILLE DE PARIS." Built 1866, by R. Napier & Sons, for the French "Compagnie Générale Transatlantique." Length, 357 ft.; breadth, 44 ft.; depth, 29 ft.; tonnage, ; horse-power, 800; speed, 15 knots.

6. Steam screw yacht, schooner rigged, "VAYNOL." Tons, B.M. 48; horse-power, 20. Built by R. Napier & Sons, 1868.

82. PHOTOGRAPH of the screw steamship "CITY OF NEW YORK" leaving the River Mersey on her voyage to New York. Built, 1866, by Tod and McGregor, Glasgow. J. Walters, Liverpool, photo., 1867.

83. PHOTOGRAPH of the screw steamship "ORION," showing the effect of a collision with another vessel, off Beachy Head, December 21, 1869. Repaired by the London Engineering and Iron Shipbuilding Company (late Westwood, Baillie, and Co.), Isle of Dogs, Poplar, 1870.

Presented by Captain Symonds, R.N. 1870.

84. Set of PHOTOGRAPHS (four in number).
Two, of R. R. Bevis' patent feathering form inboard screw propeller, fitted to screw steam yacht "KATHLEEN," by Laird Brothers.
Two Photographs of the same screw propeller, showing plan and section.

Lent by Messrs. Laird Brothers, Birkenhead. 1873.

85. PHOTOGRAPH of the Whole Model lent by H.I.H. the Prince Napoleon in 1872 of the Imperial French screw steam yacht "JEROME NAPOLEON."
See Class I., No., 12, page 13.

86. Series of DRAWINGS and PHOTOGRAPHS illustrating the following marine steam engines and boilers, steam winches, and fresh-water distilling apparatus.

Messrs. Alexander Chaplin and Co., Glasgow.
Photograph of a twin screw vertical steam engine and boiler.

CLASS XIV.—PAINTINGS AND DRAWINGS. 91

Photograph of a double cylinder screw engine with horizontal steam boiler.
Photograph of a double cylinder paddle-boat engine with vertical boiler.
Drawing on a 1 inch to 1 foot scale of steamships' winding engine, with distilling apparatus for fresh water, and steam cooking hearth.
Drawing on 6 inches to 1 foot scale of an improved donkey steam engine for feeding steam boilers with water.
Drawing on 1½ inch to 1 foot scale of a ship's improved steam winch.
The above six drawings and photographs of ships' steam apparatus presented by Messrs. Alexander Chaplin and Co., Glasgow. 1874.
See also No. 18, page 94.

87. DRAWING on a ¾ inch to 1 foot scale of an improved marine tubular steam boiler. Designed and patented by Messrs. J. and F. Howard, and made by the Barrow Shipbuilding Co., Barrow-in-Furness.
Lent by Messrs. J. and F. Howard, Engineers, Bedford.
1874.

88. DRAWING on a 1 inch to 1 foot scale of the inverted cylinder compound screw engines of the screw steamships "WINDSOR CASTLE" and "EDINBURGH CASTLE," constructed in 1872 by Messrs. R. Napier and Sons. 270 horse power, nominal.
Presented by Messrs. R. Napier and Sons, Glasgow.
1874.

89. DRAWING. Pen and ink. Port and starboard view of the figure-head of H.M.S. "Windsor Castle." Drawn by Mr. Nicholas Rundell, 1840.
Presented by Mr. J. B. Rundell. 1874.

CLASS XV.

Miscellaneous Objects and Models not comprised in the foregoing Classes.

1. Silver CLARET JUG and SALVER presented in 1858 by a company of gentlemen and engineers, to the late Sir Francis Pettit Smith, in recognition of his exertions in the application and development of the screw propeller for the propulsion of ships.
 Bequeathed by the late Sir Francis Pettit Smith.
                 1871.

2. Set of TELESCOPES formerly belonging to, and used by, Admiral Lord Nelson.
    Lent by Mr. W. H. Maitland. 1869.
 The set consists of, one 4 ft. glass; one day and night glass; one hand glass; two spare tubes, and an eye piece.

3. CAP worn by sailors on board the "INFERNAL," bomb ketch, commanded by the Hon. Capt. Perceval (Lord Egmont), at the siege of Algiers, in 1816.
    Presented by Sir. W. Trevelyan, Bart. 1869.

4. FIGURE HEAD for a ship, full size. Coloured.
 Lent by late Mr. R. Hall, 1865, now Messrs. Culmore & Long, Rotherhithe.   1874.

5. MODEL of the Eddystone Lighthouse, made by George Knott, for many years lightkeeper on the rock.
 Lent by the Corporation of the Trinity House. 1866.

6. Specimens of FISHING NETS used in the French fisheries.
    Presented by Mr. C. W. Merrifield, F.R.S. 1868.

7. A PANTAMETER, No. 1 size. For indicating the specific gravity of iron, wood, and coal, the sectional area of bars, and the cubic contents of any body that will go into the machine. Lent by Mr. A. M. Bennett. 1868.

CLASS XV.—MISCELLANEOUS OBJECTS. 93

8. Two smooth-boring AUGER BITS, recommended by the late Mr. Joseph Tucker, Joint Surveyor of H.M. Navy from 1813 to 1831, for the reduction of decay in ships.
Presented by Mr. J. S. Tucker. 1865.

9. MODEL of the JETTY, and SHEERS for masting-ships. Sheerness Dockyard. 1864.

10. MODEL. Machine for rolling bars of metal for bolts, &c.
Designed by Sir Robert Seppings, 1829. 1864.

11. Two specimens of IRON BOILER PLATE; (A) atlas iron plate; (B) best iron plate for boilers.
From the Atlas Steel and Iron Works, Sheffield. 1864.

12. Two BEARINGS fitted with white metal, which have been in use on the Great Western Railway.
J. Woods & Co. 1864.

13. ORNAMENTAL CARVED WORK, in wood, for bow and stern of ships, proposed for H.M.'s ships of the "ROYAL OAK" class, by Mr. Hellyer, carver to the Admiralty. 1860. 1864.

14. Piece of BOILER SCALE, from the steam boiler of a land engine. The specimen (polished) clearly shows the formation, and defines the adhesion to the boiler plates.
Presented by the Royal Institute of Naval Architects, per Mr. Merrifield. 1871.

15. Sectional MODEL of a Diving bell for sub-marine explorations. The Model illustrates an arrangement by Dr. John Taylor, for supplying air to the bell in an upward jet near the mouth; so that in case of the bursting of the air hose or the failure of the stop-valve (usually placed on the top of the bell) the water would only rise to the level of the air-pipe nozzle.
Presented by Dr. John Taylor, M.D., late Professor of Natural Philosophy, in the Andersonian University, Glasgow. 1874.

16. MODEL illustrating Mr. H. S. Harland's proposed apparatus for saving the lives of bathers and skaters on lakes and rivers, and showing the installation on the water side.
9 thread tarred cordage to be employed.
Presented by Mr. H. S. Harland, Brompton, Scarborough. 1874.

17. WORKING MODEL of a steam pile driving engine for submarine foundations and other work. Sissons & White's patent.
Lent by Messrs. Sissons & White, Hull. 1869.

Note.—This Model, on about ½-inch scale, is a complete working illustration of a steam pile driver. The crane to raise the monkey by an endless chain is driven by frictional gearing by the engine, which represents a high pressure inverted cylinder direct acting engine, having slide valve, eccentric, fly-wheel, and force pump for feeding the boiler with water. The boiler represents an upright tubular boiler for working at high pressure.

18. Series of DRAWINGS and PHOTOGRAPHS illustrating steam machinery manufactured by Messrs. Alexander Chaplin and Co., Glasgow.
   Photograph of a steam winding and pumping engine.
   Photograph of a steam crane.
   Photograph of a single cylinder hoisting engine.
   Photograph of a winding and pumping engine.
   Photograph of a contractor's locomotive engine.
   Drawing on a 1¼ inches to 1 foot scale of Messrs. Chaplin and Co.'s patent vertical steam boiler.
   Photograph of a travelling fresh-water distilling apparatus.

The above seven drawings and photographs presented by Messrs. Alexander Chaplin and Co., Glasgow. 1874.
See also No. 86, page 90.

19. DRAWING of Richardson's patent vertical steam boiler. Robey and Co., makers.
Lent by Messrs. Robey and Co, Lincoln. 1874.

20. DRAWING of a patent tubular upright steam boiler called the "nozzle boiler," designed and made by the Reading Ironworks Co., Limited, Reading. A 4 horse-power horizontal high-pressure steam engine.
Lent by the Reading Ironworks Co., Limited. 1874.

21. DOUBLE CYLINDER STEAM ENGINE, with two lifting and force pumps of double action. Frank Pearn and Co., makers and patentees.
Lent by Frank Pearn and Co., Engineers, Hulme Hall Road, Hulme, Manchester.

Note.—This pumping Engine, with two steam cylinders and two double-acting lifting and force pumps, will raise about 5,900 gallons of water per hour drawing 25 feet vertically. The engine has cylinders 8 inches diameter and 6-inch stroke, makes 60 revolutions per minute, and is provided with a 3-feet flywheel, governor, and 1½-inch steam pipe. The pump rams are 5 inches diameter, with a 3½-inch suction pipe.

CLASS XVI.—MISCELLANEOUS OBJECTS.

Note.—Illustrations Nos 15, 17, 18, 19, 20, 21 *being steam machinery applicable to work in connexion with the excavation and erection of harbours, docks, quays, &c., have a place in the catalogue and collection.*

22. HARBOUR LIGHT. Chance's patent Dioptric Lens of the Fourth Order, for fixed light.
  Lent by Messrs. Chance, Brothers, and Co., Glass Works, Birmingham. 1874.

23. DIAGRAMS and REGULATIONS illustrating the "rule of the road" at sea for sailing and steamships.
  By Mr. Thomas Gray, Board of Trade, 1872.

ALPHABETICAL INDEX TO SUBJECTS IN THE CATA-
LOGUE OF THE COLLECTION OF MERCANTILE
MARINE AND NAVAL MODELS IN THE SOUTH
KENSINGTON MUSEUM.

⁎ *Objects in this Index not having a page reference are
desiderata not yet in the collection.*

A.

Accessories; engine and boiler, steam. Page 54.
"Achilles;" H.M.S., 1863. Steering gear. Page 56.
"Active;" turret ship. Page 12.
Admiralty; the. Page 58.
"Agincourt;" H.M.S, 1864. Page 10.
"Ajax;" H.M.S., 1798. Page 11.
"Alabama;" corvette, of the type of. Page 27.
"Alberta;" H.M's. steam yacht, 1863. Boats. Page 58.
"A Lopez;" screw steamer, engines of. Page 49.
"Ambuscade;' H.M.S., 1773. Painting. Page 78.
"America;" 1851. Schooner, American yacht. Pages 18, 34.
"Amethyst;" H.M.S., framing of, drawing. Page 81.
Anchors; ships, ordinary and patent. Page 43.
Anderson; John S., Mr. Ice-boat. Page 63.
Appliances, ships. Page 43.
"Archimedes;" screw steamer, 1839. Coloured engravings. Pages 87, 89.
"Archimedes;" 1839. Screw steamer, 1839. Stern model. Page 51.
"Archimedes;" 1839. Screw steamer. Page 30.
Armour plated ships. Pages 10, 11, 12, 13, 14.
Armour plated ship. Dr. J. Collis Browne. Page 20.
Armour plated frigate; "Caledonia," H.M.S., 1862. Page 26.
Armour plated ship; framing of. Page 28, 29.
Armour plated ships; Laird. Bros., Messrs. Pages 15, 16.
Armour plated turret ship; Mr. Dawson. Page 13.
Armour plated ship; Messrs.Westwood, Baillie & Co. Pages 14, 26.
"Armstrong" guns. Page 66.
Arnett and Co., Messrs; sheave for blocks. Page 46.

Atkey; Pascall and Son, Messrs; fire hearths, &c. Page 42.
"Atlas" iron; specimens of. Pages 54, 93.
"Atlas" Steel and Iron Works Co. Pages 54, 72, 93.
Auger-bits; smooth boring. Mr. J. Tucker. Page 93.
"Azizea;" 1866. Turkish frigate, armour plated. Page 14.

B.

"Bahia;" gunboat. Brazilian Government, 1865. Page 15.
Balance rudders; various. Page 55.
Barometers.
"Barfleur;" H.M.S., 1762. Painting. Page 76.
Barge, state. Lord Mayor of London, 1807. Page 63.
Barges, state; see state barges.
Barges; Thames, sailing, 1855. Page 73.
"Baron Osy;" paddle steamer. Page 32.
Battan; A., Mr. Boat lowering apparatus. Page 63.
Batteries; ships of war. Pages 11, 69.
Battery; main deck. Admiral Halsted's. Page 71.
Battery; floating, three guns. Mr. Walker. Page 70.
Battery; broadside. Working of Page 69.
Beams; ships. Pages 28, 37.
Beams; construction and connecting. Pages 37, 40.
Bearings; machine, white metal. Page 93.
Bedford; Captain E., R.N., plans for buoys. Page 83.
Belaying pins. *See* pins.
Benham and Sons, Messrs. Ships' fire-hearths (cooking). Pages 41, 42.
Bennett; A. M., Mr. Pantameter. Page 92.
Berthon; E. L. Revd. Plans for collapsible ships' boats. Page 62.

G 2

Berthon; E. L., Revd. Clinometer, &c. Page 64.
Bevis; R. R., Mr. Screw propeller. Page 15.
Bevis; R. R. Screw propeller, photographs. Page 90.
Binnacles; ships' compass. Page 64.
Birch bark canoe; Hudson's Bay Territory. Page 75.
Bitts; riding and other.
Blake; R., Mr. Plans for improved ships' construction. Pages 37, 38, 39, 40.
Blake; R. Mr. Plans for ships' masts, and other improved details. Pages 41, 43, 45, 46, 56.
Blocks; ships'. Page 46.
Blocks; snatch and patent. Pages 62, 63.
Boat-hooks. [Page 58.]
Boat lowering; plans for, Clifford's. Page 63.
Boat lowering apparatus. Dr. J. C. Browne's. Page 63.
Boat lowering apparatus; Hill's. Page 63.
Boats; life. See life-boats.
Boat; pleasure, Lord Castlerosse. Page 57.
Boats; steel. Admiral Halsted's plans for. Page 57.
Boats; ships' and other. Pages 57, 58, 59, 60, 61, 62, 63.
Boats; pleasure and racing. Page 88.
Boat; fitted with two guns. Mr. Walker. Page 70.
Boat; fitted with one gun. Messrs. Laird, Bros. Page 15.
Boiler plate. Page 54.
Boilers; steam. Pages 47, 48, 91.
Boilers; cooking apparatus.
Boiler scale; steam. Page 93.
"Bolivar;" 1862. Screw steamer. Page 20.
Bollards; ships.
Bollards; gun slide. Page 69.
Bolts; ships'.
Bolts; screw and eye. Page 46.
Bonney; F. A. B., Mr. Paintings. Page 79.
Bows of ships. Page 38.
"Boyne;" 1871. Screw steamer. Page 25.
Braces; yards'. See Rigging and Rope, Yards.
Bridges; steamship; boat. Page 58.
"Brindisi;" screw steamer. Page 15.
"Britannia;" screw steamer, 1873. Page 16.
"Britannia;" 1873; screw steamer; lithograph of. Page 87.
Broker; G., Mr. Page 13.

Brotherhood and Hardingham; Messrs Photographs of steam engines, pumps, &c. Pages 50, 51.
Browne; J. Collis, Dr. Late Army Staff. Models of sailing and steam yachts, &c. Pages 20, 40, 53, 73.
Browne; J. Collis, Dr. . Life-boats. Page 63.
Bulkheads. . Pages 36, 84.
Burgoyne; Captain H. Talbot, R.N., the late. Model of "Evelyn" paddle steamer. Page 20.
Burgoyne; Captain H. Talbot, R.N., the late. Masts and rigging of H.M.S. "Ganges." Page 44.
Buss; T. O., Mr. Salinometers. Page 54.
Buttocks. Pages 33, 34.
Buttocks and waterlines. Page 33.
Buoys; life. Page 43.
Buoys; mark. Page 83.

C.

Cabins; and their fittings. Page 41.
Cables; hempen and chain. Pages 44, 47.
"Caledonia;" H.M.S., 1862. Iron-clad frigate. Page 26.
Campbell; J., Mr. Clipper ship, half model. Page 26.
Campbell; J., Mr. Ship Models. Page 18, 26.
Canoe; Cingalese. Pages 74, 75.
Canoe; Fiji or Fejee Island. Page 75.
Canoes; Hudson Bay. Page 75.
Cap; sailors'. Siege of Algiers, 1816. Page 92.
Caps; masthead. Page 45.
Capstans.
"Caroline;" screw collier. Page 32.
Carved work, wood; for ships' bow and stern. Page 93.
Casella; L. B., Mr: Ships' logs. Page 64.
"Cathay;" screw steamer, 1872. Page 25.
Catheads; anchor, fittings for.
Ceylon; boats. Page 74.
Challenger; H.M.S. Page 10.
Chance, Brothers, and Co.; Messrs.; Harbour Light. Page 95.
Chaplin; A., & Co., Messrs. Drawings and photographs of steam machinery. Pages 90, 94.
"Charkieh;" 1864. Screw steamer. Page 22.
Chart; coloured. British flags. Page 83.
Chart; flags of all nations. Ships' rigging and sails. Page 83.
Charts; navigation.

ALPHABETICAL INDEX.

"Chester;" H.M.S., 1670. Page 13.
"Cheshire;" paddle steamer. Page 18.
Chinese junks. Page 74.
Chinese boats. Page 74.
Chinese junks and boats; models of. Page 74.
Chocks.
Chocks; boat. Page 62.
Christy; T. and Co., Messrs. Drawing. Page 88.
Chronometers. Page 65.
Cingalese; outrigger canoes. See Canoe.
"City of New York;" screw steamer, 1866. Photograph. Page 90.
"City of Paris;" screw steamer, 1865. Page 19.
"City of Paris;" French mail steamer, steering gear. Page 55.
Claret jug and salver; silver. The "Smith" testimonial. Page 92.
Claxton; Capt., R.N. Oil painting. Page 79.
Cleets.
Clifford's boat-lowering apparatus. Page 63.
Clinometers. Page 64.
"Clio;" H.M.S. Page 10.
Clip hooks; patent. Dr. J. C. Browne's. Page 63.
Clipper ship; sailing. Mr. J. Campbell. Pages 18, 26.
Coble fishing; Yorkshire coast. Page 73.
Coles; Captain Cowper, R.N., the late. Iron tripod masts. Page 11.
Colomb; Capt. F., R.N. Improved ships' light. Page 65.
"Colombia;" screw steamer, 1872. Page 16.
Compasses; ships'. Page 64.
Compass; ships'. T. Gray, Liverpool. Page 64.
Compass; ships'. Napier and Sons. Page 64.
Compressors; for chain cables. Page 43.
Compressors; for guns. Page 70.
Compressor; Sir W. Symonds'. Page 43.
Congalton; Lieut. W., R.N. R. Flat surface sails. Page 44.
"Connaught;" 1860. Paddle steamer. Page 17.
"Conqueror;" H.M.S. Engines of. Page 48.
Contractor's locomotive engine; photograph. Page 94.
Construction; ships'. Iron and wood. Pages 28, 29, 30, 31, 32, 33, 34, 38, 39, 40.
Construction; iron. Pages 32, 34, 80, and 84.

Construction; wooden ship. Page 31.
Cooper; Sir Daniel, F.R.G.S. Page 75.
Cordage. See Rope.
"Cornelia;" 1868. Steam yacht. Page 26.
Corvette; of the "Alabama" class. Page 27.
Counters; engine revolution. Page 51.
Counters; speed.
Cradles; boats', H.M.S. "Orontes." Page 58.
"Cranborne;" paddle steamer, 1866. Page 16.
Crane; steam. Photographs. Page 93.
Crispin; Mrs. Boat fittings. Page 62.
"Crocodile;" H.M.S., 1866. Indian troopship. Page 14.
Crutch, metal. Page 55.
Crutches; metal. See Yoke and crutches.
Culmore and Long; Messrs. Wood carving. Page 92.
Cunard line steamship. See "Scotia."
Cunningham; H. P. D., Mr. Plans for reefing sails, &c. Page 44.
Cunningham; H. D. P., Mr. Plans for working guns. Page 69.
Cutters; sailing yachts.
Cutters; ships' boats.
"Cygnet;" sailing ship. Page 16.

D.

Daft, T. B., Mr. Sheathing. Page 30.
Dafforne; J., Mr. Model of H.M.S. "Chester," 1670. Page 13.
"Dakahlieh;" 1865. Screw steamer. Page 22.
"Dantzic;" Prussian man-of-war. Drawing. Page 82.
"Dantzic;" Prussian man-of-war. Paddle steamer. Page 32.
"Daphne;" H.M.S., 1838. Gun fitting. Page 71.
"Dauntless;" turret ship. Page 23.
Davits; boats. Page 62.
Dawson; Mr. R. Page 13.
Dead-eyes. Page 46.
"De Buffel;" Dutch armour-plated turret ship, 1868. Photograph. Page 90.
Decks, ships'. See construction.
Deck beams. See beams.
Deck planking. Page 30.
"Defence;" turret ship. Page 24.
"Delhi;" 1863. Screw steamer. Page 22.
Denny; W., and Brothers; Messrs. Pages 25, 26, 27, 49.

ALPHABETICAL INDEX.

Deptford Dockyard. Painting. Page 81.
"De Stier;" Royal Dutch Navy, 1868. Armour plated turret ship. Page 16.
"De Tyger;" Royal Dutch Navy, 1868. Armour plated turret ship. Photograph. Page 89.
Distilling apparatus; fresh water, photograph of. Pages 91, 94.
Diving apparatus.
Diving bell; sectional model of. Dr. Taylor. Page 93.
Dodd; T. F., Mr. Cingalese boats. Page 74.
Doggerbank; battle of, 1781. Painting. Page 80.
Donkey engines. Steam and Hydraulic.
Donkey engines; for feeding boilers. Page 51.
Donkey engines; for miscellaneous work.
Double boat; screw, 1823. Page 52.
Double rudder; Lieut. Hon. J. Fitzmaurice, R.N. Page 55.
Drawings. Pages 81, 82, 83, 84, 85, 86, 87, 88, 89, 91, 94.
Drawing; Mr. Lowe's ships' screws. Page 53.
Drawing; "Wyche-Lowe" 1852, and "Lowe-Harris" propellers 1862. Page 53.
Drawing; Lowe's improvements 1855; for screws. Page 53.
Drawing; "Lowe's steamship propellers." 1838. Page 53.
Drawing; Mrs. Vansittart's screw propeller. 1868. Page 53.
Drawings; Mr. Scott Russell's practical ship building. Pages 81, 82.
"Dreadnought;" turret ship. Page 11.
Drogue. Canvas floating anchor. Page 43.
"Druid" H.M.S. Page 53.
"Duke of Kent;" line-of-battle ship. Pages 11, 30.
"Duke of Kent;" line-of-battle ship. Drawing. Page 81.
"Durham;" iron sailing ship. Page 18.
Dutch Galiot. 1774. Page 19.
Dutch shipping; painting. Pages 80, 81.
Dutch men-of-war; painting. Page 80.

E.

"Eagle;" screw collier. Page 32.
"Eddystone" lighthouse; model of. Page 92.

Edinburgh; His Royal Highness the Duke of. Models of ships, boats, &c. Pages 10, 57, 75, 87.
"Edinburgh Castle;" screw steamer, drawing of engines. Page 91.
Edye; J., Mr. Plans for fitting guns. Page 71.
Edwardes; T. Dyer, Mr. Paintings, &c. Pages 80, 81, 83.
Egypt; Viceroy of, the. Sailing yacht, Nile boat. Page 74.
Egyptian Commissioner, Paris Exhibition; 1867. Sailing yacht, Nile boat. Page 74.
Engines. See steam engines.
Engravings, &c. Page 83.
Engraving; coloured buoys, marks. Page 83.
Engravings; ships of war of ancient date. Page 83.
"Enterprize;" H.M.S. 1774. Painting. Page 78.
"Elgin;" H.M.'s steam yacht. 1849. Boats. Page 58.
Elliott, Admiral George. Page 25.
"Empire;" American river paddle steamer. Page 74.
Esquimaux canoe; Hudson's Bay Territory. Page 75.
"Euphrates;" H.M.S. Indian troopship. 1866. Page 14.
"Evelyn;" 1864. Paddle steamer. Page 20.
Experiment; H.M.S. 1774. Painting. Page 78.
"Excellent;" H.M.S. Gun fittings. Page 69.

F.

Faggot built masts. Page 45.
"Fairy;" H.M.'s steam yacht. 1852. Boats. Page 58.
"Faraday;" screw steamer. 1874. Telegraph ship. Page 21.
Fawcus; George, Mr. Plans for lifeboats, patent blocks, &c. Pages 62, 83.
Fids and fidding; masts. Page 45.
"Fiery Cross:" 1855. Clipper sailing ship. Page 26.
"Fiery Cross;" 1861. Clipper sailing ship. Page 18.
Figure-head; ships'. Wood carving for. Page 91.
Figure-head; ships'. Drawing. Page 91.
Fiji island, boats.
"Fiji;" double sailing canoe. Page 75.
Fire engines.
Fire-hearths; ships' cooking. Pages 41, 42.
Fishing boats. Page 73.

ALPHABETICAL INDEX. 101

Fishing nets. Page 92.
Fittings, ships'. Page 41.
Fittings for shrouds; ships. Page 46.
Fitzmaurice; Hon. J., Lieut. Plan for rudder. Page 55.
Flat-surface sails. Page 44.
Floors; ships'. Page 37, 38.
Floor timbers. Pages 39, 40.
Fog horn. Page 65.
Forecastle; ships'.
Forecastle, ships', gun. Page 70.
Foreign craft and vessels. Page 74.
Fore topsail of Nelson's ship "Victory." 1805. Photograph. Page 89.
"Formidable;" turret ship. Page 24.
Forrest and Son; Messrs. Ships' and pleasure boats. Pages 59, 60.
Forrester; G., and Co.; Messrs. Models of engines. Page 49.
Foster; A. J. Revd. Nile boat. Page 75.
Fothergill; P. A. Revd. Screw propellers. Page 51.
Four-masted screw steamer. Painting. Page 82.
Frames and framing of ships. Pages 38, 39.
Framing; ships'. Page 28.
Fresh-water distilling apparatus; photographs of. Pages 91, 94.
Frigates; armour clad, Turkish. Pages 14, 90.
Frigate; armour plated. R. Griffiths'. Page 13.
Frost, Brothers; Messrs. Cordage & Rope. Page 47.
Futtocks. Page 38.
Fuzes; gunnery, metal and wood. Page 67.

G.

"Galatea;" steam yacht, 1867. Page 14.
Galiot, Dutch; 1774. Page 19.
"Ganges;" H.M.S., 1830. Page 44.
Gauges. See Pressure gauges. Page 54.
Gauges. See Water gauges, for boilers and condensers.
Gauges. See Vacuum gauges.
Gauges. See Wind gauges.
Gibson; T. D. E. Mr. Ceylon boat. Page 74.
Gisborne; J. S., Mr.
"Glen" line steamships; models of. Page 21.
"Glengyle;" paddle steamer. Page 27.
Godlee; Burwood, Mr. Propeller model. Page 52.
"Golconda;" 1863. Screw steamer. Page 23.

Governors; engine.
Gray, John, Mr. Compass & binnacle Page 64.
Gray; Thomas, Mr. "Rules of the road." Page 94.
Gray; William, Mr. Marine boilers. Pages 50, 51.
"Great Britain;" screw steamer. Page 52.
"Great Britain;" screw steamer ashore, 1847, painting. Page 79.
"Great Eastern;" steamship, 1857. Models, paintings, and drawings of. Pages 40, 81, 82, 84, 85, 86.
Griffiths; R., Mr. Double screw ship of war. Page 13.
Guns; ships'. Pages 11, 66, 69, 70.
Guns. See Armstrong, Whitworth, and Woolwich guns.
Guns and carriages; ships'. Page 11.
Gunboats; steam. Laird, Bros. Messrs. Page 15.
Gunboat; Mr. Tucker. Page 70.
Gunboat; Mr. H. P. D. Cunningham. Page 69.
Gun; brass, ships'; old pattern. Page 71.
Gun carriages, wood; naval pattern. Pages 70, 71.
Gun carriages, iron; naval pattern.
Gun, fitted; H.M.S. "Rapid." Page 71.
Gun carriages; modern naval. Page 71.
Gun carriages; iron. Capt. T. B. Heathorn's. Pages 11, 69.
Gunwales. Page 58.
"Gwalior;" 1873, screw steamer. Page 25.

H.

Half block models Page 22.
Halsted; Admiral E. Pellew. The late. Pages 11, 23, 31, 36, 57, 71.
Halyards; flag or signal. See Rope and cordage.
Harbour Light, fixed. Page 95.
Hardie; J., Revd. Pages 37, 38, 39, 44, 41, 43, 45, 46, 56, 71.
Hardwicke; the Earl of, model of H.M.S. "Ajax," 1798. Page 11.
Harland; H. S., Mr. Life apparatus. Pages 43, 93.
Harrison; G., Mr. M. I. C. E. Steam ferry boat. Page 18.
Harvey; D., Mr. Pages 61, 64.
Hawse-holes; hawse pipes.
Hawsers. See Rope.
Hawthorn; R. and W., Messrs. Boiler model, &c. Page 50.

ALPHABETICAL INDEX.

Head board; ships'. Page 40.
Heathorn; Capt., T. B., R. A. Pages 11, 71.
"Heiligerlee;" Royal Dutch Navy, 1868. Armour-plated turret ship. Page 15.
"Helen McGregor;" engines of paddle steamer, 1845. Page 49.
"Hibernian;" screw steamer. Page 19.
Hill, E. J., Mr. Boat lowering apparatus. Page 63.
Hill and Clark, Messrs. Boat lowering apparatus and slip hooks. Page 63.
Hoisting engine; photograph. Page 94
Hooks. *See* Slip and clip hooks.
Hooper and Nickson; Messrs. Page 30.
Horse stalls; on board ship. Page 41.
Howard; J. and F., Messrs. Page 91.
Hudson's Bay Company; The. Page 75.
Humphrys and Tennant; Messrs. Engine models. Page 48.
Hurst; Capt. J. W., life rafts. Page 58, 62.
"Hydrostatic" steering apparatus; Admiral Inglefield's. Page 56.
"Hysdaspes," screw steamer, 1874. Page 25.

I.

Ice boat; "Falcon." Page 63.
"Idaho;" 1868, screw steamer. Page 26.
"Imogen;" H.M.S. 1831, gun fitting. Page 71.
Indian rivers; steamers for. Pages 16, 17.
Inglefield; Admiral, E. A. C. B. Steering apparatus. Page 56.
Inman; William, Mr. Page 19.
Inman Steamship Company; The. Models of steamships. Page 19.
"Intrepid;" H.M.S., 1770. Painting. Page 77.
Instruments for navigation; Page 64.
Ironclad ships.
Ironclad ships; Admiral Halsted's. Page 11.
Iron screw steamer; Baltic trader. Page 17.
"Irrawaddy;" 1874, screw steamer. Page 25.

J.

James Lowe;" screw steamer. Page 52.
Jerome Napoleon;" steam yacht. French. Page 13.

"Jerome Napoleon;" steam yacht. Photograph. Page 90.
Jetty and sheers. Sheerness Dockyard. Page 93.
"Jumna;" paddle steamer. 1832. Page 17.
"Jumna;" H.M.S. 1866. Indian troopship. Page 14.
Junks and boats; Chinese. Models of. Page 74.

K.

"Kala-fish;" schooner yacht. Dr. J. C. Browne. Pages 20, 73.
"Kate;" yawl. E. Middleton, Esq. Page 60.
Keels; ships'. Page 28.
Keel blocks. Page 39.
Kennedy; John, Mr. Plan for shipbuilding and screw propellers. Page 31.
"Kingfisher;" H.M.S., 1770. Painting. Page 79.
"Konig Wilhelm;" German armourplated ship. 1869. Page 20.
Kullberg; Victor. Chronometers. Page 65.

L.

Ladd; W., Mr. Plans for ship fittings, &c. Pages 62, 74, 75.
"Lady Daly;" life boat. Page 57.
"Lady Daly;" life boat. Lithograph of. Page 87.
Laird Brothers; Messrs. Pages 15, 17, 87, 90.
Lamb and White; Messrs. Boats. Page 58.
Lamps. *See* Lights.
"Lancashire Witch;" steam yacht. Page 15.
Lanterns; ships'. See Lights.
Lapraike; D., Mr. Model of American steamer "Empire." Page 74.
"Lapwing;" screw steam yacht. Dr. J. Collis Browne. Page 54.
Launches; ships' boats.
Launches; steam.
Launch of a frigate at Millwall; drawing. Page 82.
Launch at Deptford Dockyard; painting. Page 81.
Laurence Hill & Co.; Messrs. Iron ship "Victory," 1863. Page 27.
Lay; W. T., Mr. Model of a Chinese junk. Page 74.
"Laying off;" steam frigate. Drawing of. Pages 28.
Lead lines. Page 65.
Leads; sounding.

ALPHABETICAL INDEX. 103

"Leinster ;" 1860. Engines of paddle steamer. Page 49.
Lepanto; battle of, 1571. Painting. Page 80.
"Le Sceptre ;" French ship-of-war, 1700. Page 13.
"Liberty ;" H.M.S. Gun fitting. Page 72.
Life-boats. Pages 57, 58, 59, 60, 61, 62, 63.
Life-boats. Engraving of Fawcus's. Page 83.
Life-buoys.
Life-buoys; stowage of, Mr. H. S. Harland. Page 43.
Life-rafts.
Life-rafts; Capt. Hurst's. Pages 58, 62.
Life-saving apparatus.
Live-saving apparatus ; Mr. H S. Harland's. Page 93.
Lightning conductors. Page 47.
Lighthouse; the Eddystone. Page 92.
Lighthouses.
Lights; harbour and coast. Page 95.
Lights; ships'. Pages 64, 65.
Light ships.
Light ships. Trinity House, on "Goodwin" sands. Page 16.
Lines; ships'. Pages 31 to 36; 83 to 87.
Lithographs ; illustrating practical shipbuilding. Pages 83 to 87.
Logs; ships'. Ordinary and patent. Page 64.
Log-lines. See Rope and Cordage.
"Lombardy ;" screw steamer, 1873. Page 25.
"Lopez A. ;" screw steamer. See "A. Lopez."
"Lord W. Bentinck ;" paddle steamer, 1832. Page 17.
Lowe ; A. T., Mr. Model of sailing ship. Page 16.
Lowe; J., Mr. Screw propellers. Pages 52, 53.
"Lowe, James ;" screw boat, 1838. Page 52.
Lubricators; engine. Page 54.
Lumley; H., Mr. Rudders. Pages 55, 83.

M.

Magazines; ships' powder.
"Magna ;" paddle steamer. 1832. Page 17.
Maitland ; W. H., Mr. Telescopes, Lord Nelson's. Page 92.
"Malabar ;" H.M.S., 1866. Indian troop ship. Photograph. Page 89.
"Maltese" men-of-war; at anchor. Painting. Page 80.

Maltese and Algerine Vessels, in action. Painting. Page 80.
Maltese galley. Fighting galley. Page 80.
Maltese galley. Painting of. Page 80.
"Marianne ;" Nile boat. Page 75.
Marine boilers. Page 50.
Marine boilers ; high pressure. Model and drawing of. Page 50.
Marine engines. See Engines.
Marine steam boilers. See Boilers.
Martin ; Claude, Mr. Anchors and cables ; patent. Page 43.
"Mary White ;" life-boat. Page 59.
Masts; ships'. Pages 44, 45.
Masts. See Tripod masts.
Masts for ships of war ; Mr. Blake's. Page 45.
Masts ; faggot built, for warships. Mr. Tucker. Page 45.
"Mataban ;" 1874. Screw steamer. Page 25.
Maudslay, Sons, and Field; Messrs. Page 17.
McCool; J., Mr. Plans for stopping holes. Page 36.
McGregor, Gow, & Co.; Messrs. Steamship models. Page 21.
"Medway ;" screw steamer. Page 17.
Men-of-war in port. Painting. Page 80.
Merrifield; C. W., Mr. Plans for rudders. Page 55.
Merrifield ; C. W., Mr. Specimens of fishing nets. Pages 92, 93.
Messenger ; T., Mr. Improved boiler. Page 50.
Metal sheathing. See Sheathing.
Metal fuzes ; gunnery. See Fuzes.
Midship sections. See Sections.
Midship section ; Admiral Halsted's ships. Page 31.
Millwall Iron Works Company; Model of H.M.S. "Northumberland," &c. Pages 11, 18.
"Minotaur ;" H.M.S., 1863. Page 10.
Miscellaneous models. Page 92.
"Monarch ;" H.M.S., 1868. Engines of. Page 48.
"Montana ;" screw steamer, 1873. Page 15.
Moorings.
"More Vane ;" steam yacht, 1869. Page 15.
Mortar bed; gunnery. Page 70.
"Mule" fishing ; Yorkshire coast. Page 73.
Murray; Andrew, Mr. Model of steering wheel. Page 55.

N.

Napier; R. & Sons, Messrs. Armour-plated ships, &c. Pages 11, 14, 19, 23, 24, 31, 37, 55, 57, 71, 89, 91.
Napier and Sons; Messrs. R. Guns, ships'. Page 71.
Napier; D., & Sons, Messrs. Patent compass. Page 64.
Napoleon; H.I.H. the Prince. Model of screw yacht. Pages 13, 90.
National Life-boat Institution. See Royal.
"Nautilus" propellers; screw. Page 31.
Nautochometers. Page 64.
Navigation; instruments for. Page 64.
"Nelson;" H.M.S., 18. Engines of. Page 48.
"Nevada;" 1868. Screw steamer. Page 26.
Newall & Co.; Messrs. Wire rope. Page 47.
"Niagara;" steering wheel, of steamer. Page 55.
Nile; boats. Pages 74, 75.
"Nix;" Prussian gunboat, paddle wheel. Lines of. Page 34.
"Nix;" Prussian gun-boat, paddle wheel. Drawing of. Page 82.
"Northumberland;" H.M.S., 1866. Page 10.
"Norwegian;" screw steamer. Page 19.
"Novelty;" 1840. Screw steamer. Pages 30, 51.
"Nyanza;" 1864. Paddle steamer. Page 23.
"Nyzam;" 1873. Screw steamer. Page 25.

O.

Oars. [Page 58.]
"Orion;" screw steamer. Photograph. Page 90.
"Orkhanea;" 1866. Turkish armour-plated frigate. Page 14.
"Orontes;" H.M's. troopship, 1862. Boats. Page 58.
'Osborne;" H.M's. steam yacht, 1843. Boats. Page 58.
"Osmanea;" 1866. Turkish armour-plated frigate. Page 14.
"Osman," "Ghazy;" Turkish armour-plated frigates. Photographs. Page 90.
Oswald and Co., Messrs.; iron ships. Steamships. Page 17.
"Outrigger;" eight-oared racing boat. Page 63.

P.

"Pacific;" paddle steamer. Page 32.
"Pacific;" paddle steamer, drawing of. Page 82.
"Pacific;" engines of paddle steamship, drawing of. Page 82.
Paddle engines. Page 49.
Paddle engines; J. Scott Russel, Esq. Page 49, 82.
Paddle engines; Ravenhill, Easton & Co., Messrs. Page 48.
Paddle wheels. Pages 19, 49.
Paddle wheel steamer; trader, drawing. Page 85.
Page; W. R., Mr. Cingalese canoe. Page 75.
Paintings. Page 76.
Paintings on copper. Page 79.
"Palmer's Shipbuilding Company, Limited." Models of steam ships. Pages 14, 15, 26.
Pantameter. Page 92.
Pearn; Frank, and Co. Steam pumping engine. Page 94.
Peninsular and Oriental Steam Navigation Company; the. Models of steam ships. Pages 22, 23.
"Pereire;" screw steamer, 1866. Photograph. Page 90.
Photographs. Page 89.
Pile drivers; ordinary and steam. Page 94.
Pilot boats. Page 73.
Pinnaces; (boats).
Pins; belaying, thole, and other.
Plenty and Sons; Messrs. Screw engines, &c. Pages 50, 51.
Pontoon train; Fawcus's. Page 62.
Pontoon; iron. For raising wrecks, lithograph. Page 88.
Ports; ships. Page 41.
Ports; plans for barring in. Page 41.
Port; gun. Page 39.
"Portland;" H.M.S., 1770, painting. Page 77.
"Powerful;" turret ship. Page 23.
Pressure gauges; see steam, water, and vacuum gauges.
Pressure gauges; steam, for boilers. See gauges.
"Prince Albert;" H.M.S. 1864, engines of. Page 48.
Projectiles. Pages 66, 72.
Projectiles, "Whitworth." Pages 67, 68.
Propulsion of ships; methods for. Pages 48, 51.
Propulsion of boats; models for the. Pages 49, 52.

ALPHABETICAL INDEX. 105

Pumping engines. Page 94.
Pumps; ships'.
Pybus, J., Mr. Model of Chinese junks and boats. Page 74.

Q.

Queen, Her Majesty The. Paintings. Pages 76 to 79.

R.

Racing and pleasure boats; drawings of. Page 88.
"Racoon;" H.M.S. 1857. Page 10.
"Rapid;" H.M.S. gun fitting. Page 71.
Ratchet and lever; setting up shrouds Blake's. Page 46.
Ravenhill, Easton, and Co.; Messrs. Models of marine engines. Pages 48, 49.
Reading Ironworks Co.; the. Drawing of steam boiler. Steam-engine. Page 94.
Reed; E. J., Esqre. C.B. M.P. Page 21.
Reefing sails, from the deck; mode of. Page 44.
Reynolds; James, Mr. British and other flags, chart of. Page 83.
Riders; external iron. See "Caledonia" H.M.S.
Rigging; ships. Page 44.
Robey and Co.; Messrs. Drawing of steam boiler. Page 94.
Rolling machine; for iron bolts. Page 93.
Rope; specimens of for rigging, &c. Pages 47, 65.
Rope. See wire rope. Page 47.
"Rouen;" paddle steamer. Pages 32, 33.
Royal National Life-boat Institution. Model of life-boat and carriage Page 60.
"Royal Oak;" H.M.S. 1769. Painting. Page 77.
"Royal George;" H.M.S. 1756. Painting. Page 76.
Royal West India Mail Steamships. Painting. Page 82.
Rudders. Pages 55, 56, 83.
Rudders; permanent and temporary. Pages 55, 56.
Rudders; see balance rudders.
"Rules of the road;" at sea. Page 94.
Rundell; J.B., Mr. Drawing. Page 91.
Russell; John Scott, Mr. Models. Pages 18, 31 to 36, 49.
Russell; John Scott, Mr. Drawings illustrating practical shipbuilding. Pages 83 to 87.

S.

Sailing ship, four masted. In gale of wind. Drawing. Page 82.
Sails; ships. Page 44.
"Salamander;" Prussian gunboat, paddle-wheel, lines of. Page 34.
"Salamander;" Prussian gunboat. Drawing. Page 82.
Salimometers; for boilers. Page 54.
"Santa Rosa;" screw steamer, 1872. Page 16.
Schäffer & Budenberg, Messrs; steam accessories. Page 54.
"Scotia;" 1861. Iron paddle steamer. (Cunard line.) Page 18.
Screw collier; J. Scott Russell's. Page 32.
Screw engines. Pages 48, 49, 50.
Screw engines; Plenty and Sons, Messrs. Page 50.
Screw engines; Verey and Lange, Messrs. Page 50.
Screw propellers. Pages 51, 52, 53.
Screw propeller; Bevis's; photographs of. Page 90.
Screw propeller; Dr. J. Collis Browne's, patent. Page 53.
Screw propellers; Revd. J. Fothergill's patent. Page 51.
Screw propellers; the "Nautilus." Page 31.
Screw propeller; J. Lowe's patent, 1838. Page 52.
Screw propeller ¼ scale; "Lowe-Vansittart." 1868. Page 53.
Screw propeller; model of old. Page 52.
Screw boss, oval; J. Lowe's, 1855 Page 52.
Screw boss, spherical; J. Lowe's, 1852. Page 52.
Screw shaft and boss; J. Lowe's, 1838. Page 52.
Screw steamer; "Britannia," drawing of. Page 87.
Screw steamer; drawing of. Page 82.
Screw steamer; trader. Pages 32, 33.
Screw steamer; small trader. Page 32.
Screw steamer; Capt. A. Thompson's design for. Pages 40, 88.
Sculls. See oars.
Scuppers.
Searle and Sons; Messrs. Models of a sailing barge. Page 73.
Searle and Sons; Messrs. Pleasure and racing boats. Pages 57, 63.
Searle and Sons; Messrs; pleasure boats, drawings of, &c. Page 88.
Sections; midship and other. Pages 28, 29, 31.
Self-reefing topsails. Page 44.

Seppings; Sir Robert. Iron rolling machine. Page 93.
"Serapis;" H.M.S. 1866. Indian troopship. Page 14.
Sextants.
Shackles; chain cable.
Shackle; gun. Page 72.
Sheathing; ship's, plans for. Page 30.
Sheathing; wood. Page 30.
Sheathing; zinc. Page 30.
Shells, &c. for guns. Pages 66, 68.
Sheers; masting. Page 93.
Ships' boats. Page 57.
Shipbuilding; iron. Lloyds' register rules. Page 87.
Shipping; painting of. Page 80.
Ship's forecastle; fitted with gun pivots and racers. Page 70.
Ships' lights. *See* Lights:—
Shot proof shields.
Shot and shell; gunnery. Pages 66, 72.
Shrouds; method of securing. Page 46.
Siebe and Gorman; Messrs. Page 88.
Siemens; C. W., Dr., F.R.S. Page 21.
Signal flags.
Signal lights. *See* lights.
Silber Light Co., the; ships' lights and lamps. Page 65.
Sissons and White; Messrs. Page 94.
Slip hooks; Dr. J. C. Browne's. Page 63.
Slip hooks; Mr. J. Fawcus'. Page 62.
Slip hooks; Mr. R. Blakes'. Page 43.
Slip hooks; Mr. Hills'. Page 63.
Small stores; gun. Page 70.
Smith; George, Mr. Page 81.
Smith; Sir F. Pettit, the late. The "Smith" testimonial. Page 92.
Snatch blocks; Mr. J. Fawcus'. Page 62.
Snatch blocks; Mr. R. Blake. Page 43.
Solebay; battle of, 1672. Painting. Page 80.
"Sovereign of the Seas." 1637. English man-of-war. Pencil drawing of. Page 81.
"Sovereign of the Seas," 1637. English man-of-war. Engraving.
Speed indicators. *See* Logs and counters.
"Sphinx;" H.M.S., 1775. Painting. Page 79.
Starnes; J. S., Mr.; Ships' lights. Page 65.
State barges; Admiralty. Page 58.
State barge, 1807. Lord Mayor of London. Page 63.
Stays, masts.' *See* rigging.
Steam boilers. *See* Boilers.
Steam engines. Pages 48, 49, 50, 90.
Steam engines. *See* donkey, paddle, and screw engines.

Steam gauges. *See* gauges or pressure gauges.
Steel boats, ships'. Admiral Halsted's. Page 57.
Steering apparatus. Page 55.
Steering apparatus. "Hydrostatic. Page 56.
Steering gear. Page 55.
Steering wheel; the "Niagara," 1857. Page 55.
Steers; Mr., New York. Pages 18, 34.
Steps of lower masts. Page 46.
Stern of screw steamer. 1838. Pages 30, 51.
Stern; oval. Mr. Tucker. Page 30.
Sterns of screw ships. Pages 51, 52.
Sterns of ships. Blake's plans. Page 38.
Sterns of ships construction. Pages 30, 38.
Stevens and Sons; Messrs. Ships' lights. Page 64.
Stoppers; chain cable. Page 43.
Stoppers; shot hole.
Stopper bolts. Page 41.
Stopping holes; plans for. Page 36.
Stoves; ships'. Page 42.
Stoves, cabin.
Stoves. See firehearths.
Strake and gunwale; boats'. Page 58.
"Surat;" 1866. Screw steamer. Page 22.
Sweeps. See oars.
Symonds; Capt., R. N. Photograph. Page 90.
Symonds; Sir W. Page 43.

T.

Tacks and sheets; sails'. See rigging and rope for.
"Tamar;" H.M.S. 1863. Engines of. Page 48.
"Tanjore;" 1865. Screw steamer. Page 20.
Taylor; Dr. John, M.D. Page 34, 93.
Telegraph apparatus; engine-room and steering.
Telescopes.
Telescopes; Lord Nelson's. Page 92.
"Themis;" sailing yacht. Page 34.
Thimble; gun. Page 72.
Thimbles.
Thomson; Capt. A. Screw steamer. Pages 40, 88.
Thomson; Mr. A. Pages 40, 88.
Timbers; ships'. Page 37.
"Titania;" sailing yacht. Page 34.
Toggles. Pages 43, 44, 46.
Topmasts and top-gallant masts. *See* masts.
Top masts and top-gallant masts; ordinary.

ALPHABETICAL INDEX. 107

Topmast; patent, Capt. Turnbull. Page 45.
Topsails; ordinary and patent. Page 44.
Tops; mast.
Transports.
Transports; fittings for. Page 41.
Traversing gear; gun. Page 69.
Tree canoe; Hudson bay territory. Page 75.
Trevelyan; Sir W., Bart. Sailors cap, siege of Algiers, 1816. Page 92.
Trinity House; Corporation of the. Models. Pages 14, 17, 92.
Tripod masts. Page 11.
Troop ships. Page 14.
Tucker; Joseph, Mr. Design for line of battle ship, &c. Pages 29, 30, 81.
Tucker; J. Scott, Mr. Models of ships. Drawings, &c. Pages 11, 29, 30, 45, 55, 70, 81, 93.
Tucker; John Scott, Mr. Ships' sections. Fittings, &c. Pages 29, 30, 55.
Tumbler hooks; Blake's. Page 45.
Turnbull, Capt. Patent topmast. Page 45.
Turnbull; T., Mr., A.I.N.A. Boats, Whitby. Page 73.
Turner; George, Mr. Plans for armourplated ships. Pages 12, 13, 26, 27.
Turner; George, Mr. Plans for lifeboats. Page 61.
Turret ships; models of. Admiral Halsted's. Page 11, 23, 24.
Turret ships; models of. Laird, Bros. Messrs. Pages 15, 16.
Turret ship; model of. Westwood and Baillie, Messrs. Page 26.
Turret ship; Mr. R. Dawson's. Page 13.
Turret ships; section of. Admiral Halsted's. Page 31.
Turrets; gun. Pages 69, 71.
Turret; gun boat. Cunningham's. Page 69.

U.

"Undine;" sailing yacht. Page 34.

V.

Vacuum gauges; engine. Page 54. See gauges.
Vanes; wind.
Vansittart, Henrietta, Mrs.; Screw propellers. Pages 52, 53.
"Vaynol;" screw steam yacht, 1868. Photograph. Page 90.

"Vedette;" turret ship. Page 12.
"Venetia;" 1873. Screw steamer. Page 25.
"Venezuelan;" 1865, screw steamer. Page 19.
Ventilation, ships'; Page 41.
Verey and Lange, Messrs; screw engines. Page 49.
"Victoria and Adelaide;" screw steamer. Page 35.
"Victoria and Albert;" 1855. II.M.S. steam yacht. Boats. Page 58.
"Victory;" H.M.S., 1737. Painting Page 76.
"Victory;" Lord Nelson's ship. Foretopsail of. Photograph. Page 89.
"Victory;" 1863. Iron sailing ship. Page 27.
"Vigilant;" turret ship. Page 24.
"Ville de Paris;" 1866. Screw steamer. Photograph. Page 90.
Screw steering gear. Page 55.

W.

Wales, of ships. Pages 33, 38.
Walker, J., Mr.; ships' batteries, &c. Page 70.
Walker, J., Mr.; ship construction. Page 29.
"Warren;" American packet ship. Painting. Page 81.
"Warrior;" H.M.S., 1860. Armourplating for, plans by J. Scott Russell. Page 35.
Washing apparatus.
Water closets.
Water gauges; for boilers and condensers.
Waterlines, ships'. Whole and half block models. Pages 34, 35, 36.
"Waterwitch;" H.M.S., 1866. Page 25.
Wave lines. Pages 31, 32, 33, 34, 83, 84, 85, 86, 87.
"Wave Queen;" paddle steam yacht. Page 33.
Ways; launching. Page 16.
West India and Pacific, steam shipping Company. The Models of steamships. Pages 19, 20.
Westwood, Baillie & Co.; Messrs. Pages 14, 26.
Whitby, boats. Page 73.
Whitby, fishing boats, 5 man. Page 73.
White; J., and Co. Messrs. Boats. Page 59.
White; J., and Co. Messrs. Lamb and White's boats. Page 58.
White; J. G., Mr. Propeller for shallow water. Page 48.

Whitworth; Sir Joseph, Bart. Guns and projectiles. Pages 11, 68.
Whitworth; Armoury Company. Projectiles, &c. Pages 67, 68.
"Whitworth" guns. Pages 11, 68.
Whole Models. Pages 10, 19.
Willcocks; S., Mr. Photograph. Page 89.
Wilson; A. and Co., Messrs. Donkey engine and pump. Page 51.
Wimshurst; H., Mr. Construction, &c. Pages 30, 51.
Wimshurst; H., Mr. Lithographs. Page 87.
Winches; steam and ordinary. Page 90.
Wind gauges.
Windlasses.
"Windsor Castle;" screw steamship. Drawing of engines. Page 91.
"Windsor Castle;" H.M.S. Figurehead, drawing of. Page 91.
Wire rope. Page 47.

Wood fuzes; gunnery. *See* Fuzes.
Woods; J and Co. Messrs. White metal for machine bearings. Page 93.
"Woolwich" gun; Naval muzzle loading. Page 66.
"Wyvern;" H.M.S., 1864. Armour clad ship. Page 16.

Y.

Yachts; sailing and steam, &c. Pages 33, 34.
Yacht; rigged. Viceroy of Egypt's, Nile, 1867. Page 74.
Yacht; sailing. Lines of. Pages 34, 35.
Yacht; steam screw, Dr. J. C. Browne's. Page 20.
Yard's; ships'.
Yards; plans for bracing the. Page 44.
Yawls. *See* Boats.
Yawls. *See* Yachts.
Yoke and crutches; boats. Page 62.

LONDON:
Printed by GEORGE E. EYRE and WILLIAM SPOTTISWOODE,
Printers to the Queen's most Excellent Majesty.
For Her Majesty's Stationery Office.
[P. 1903a.—500.—11/74.]

www.ingramcontent.com/pod-product-compliance
Lightning Source LLC
Chambersburg PA
CBHW031403160426
43196CB00007B/877